MAKE MONEY ONLINE FROM HOME

DROP SHIPPING, AFFILIATE MARKETING,
SELLING EBOOKS, NETWORK MARKETING,
WEBSITE FLIPPING, BITCOIN TRADING, FOREX,
BLOGGER, WEB DEVELOPMENT AND
CREATING ANIMATION VIDEO

2 BOOK IN 1

DIEGO DE GIOVANNI

TABLE OF CONTENTS

MAKE MONEY FROM HOME PASSIVE INCOME 2020

THE SECRET OF MAKING MONEY PASSIVELY FROM DROP SHIPPING, AFFILIATE MARKETING, SELLING EBOOKS, NETWORK MARKETING AND WEBSITE FLIPPING

DIEGO DE GIOVANNI

Disclaimer

All erudition contained in this book is given for informational and educational purposes only. The author is not in any way accountable for any results or outcomes that emanate from using this material. Constructive attempts have been made to provide information that is both accurate and effective, but the author is not bound for the accuracy or use/misuse of this information.

Foreword

First, I will like to thank you for taking the first step of trusting me and deciding to purchase/read this life-transforming eBook. Thanks for spending your time and resources on this material.

I can assure you of exact results if you will diligently follow the exact blueprint, I lay bare in the information manual you are currently reading. It has transformed lives, and I strongly believe it will equally transform your own life too.

All the information I presented in this Do It Yourself piece is easy to digest and practice.

INTRODUCTION

The discovery of passive income opportunities in 2019 stands out from the solutions to accumulate the different salary increases necessary to remain financially sufficient in the current economy. The "new economy" that currently operates in the United States has proven to be a performer of the vocation, wages, and lifestyle of middle-class Americans. The ultimate effect of this amazing truth, as obvious as it may be, is that most of us must recognize a total change of perspective from our experience of the last forty years and adapt to it. We can never rely solely on work to meet our sustainable needs for money. The appropriate response is to create our own "backup plan" by building multiple sources of payment from different sources. Automated revenue openings are an ideal answer because they require a minimal measure of your chances of working. As a result, companies that rely on automated revenue openings can grow despite their normal daily employment.

CHAPTER ONE
THE TRUE DEFINITION
OF PASSIVE INCOME

If you search the internet for "passive income", you may find a definition or two, but mostly, what you find are websites trying to sell you on the passive-income-flavor-of-the-day. It's frustrating, I know. I don't know about you, but before I jump into any opportunity or even before I take a trip, I like to do my research. That being said, there are a lot of good opportunities out there. But before you start spending money, let's discuss what passive income is and, most importantly, what it isn't.

Webster's dictionary defines passive income as "of, relating to, or being business activity in which the investor does not have immediate control over income". I don't think that tells the whole story. Passive income is money that you receive over and over again without having to do much work (notice I didn't say "any work"). It is different than earned income in that you are not receiving money for your time (like you would a job). But depending on the passive income stream that you choose, you may in fact have immediate control over your income. But I'll get to that later.

Why would you want passive income? Well, like Robert Kiyosaki explains in his book Rich Dad Poor Dad, that is the main difference between the rich and the middle class. The rich invest their money in various passive income streams. When their passive income exceeds their expenses, then they are financially free. "Financially free" simply means that you do not have to have a day job to pay your expenses. And you are "free" to then do whatever you want!

What Passive Income Isn't

Before I go into telling you what passive income is, let me first tell you want it isn't. Passive income is not the same thing as "residual income". Residual income is money that you receive on a regular basis after having done work once. The best example would be TV sitcoms. Some actors get "residuals". Actors get paid for filming the show. Afterwards, some actors get paid each time the show repeats. Sales people that sell services, subscriptions, or renewable products (like insurance) sell that item once and, providing the customer renews, will get a commission off of each renewal. Royalties from the sale of books and music are also residual.

Many say that multi-level-marketing or network marketing sales provide you with passive income. Guess what? That's residual too.

If you have a small business or are self-employed, even if you are making a lot of money, this is NOT passive income. If you receive a salary from your business, that is earned income. There is a way to turn this into passive income, however - so stay tuned.

You know, I have to say that starting your own website cannot be passive income. Whether you are selling a product (such as an eBook, seminar or other information) or a service, you still have to market your website. You will have to do this regardless of whether you are selling your OWN products or have the rights to sell other's products. Marketing your website is work, simple as that. But it's not a job. And once your marketing efforts start taking off, you can make a lot of money with little additional effort. But that is residual in my book, not passive.

What Passive Income IS

Passive income is a lot of things. The first thing that comes to mind, and also, I believe, the most popular example is real estate. If you own investment property and are getting a positive cash flow from a house, commercial property, or apartment, that is passive income. If you rent rooms in your house, that's passive income too. You only have to set this up once, and then the income comes in month after month. Interest income from savings accounts, CDs, and money-market accounts are passive - the bank pays you for keeping your money in those accounts. If you have a website with banner ads or Google AdSense ads, that can be called passive as well.

If you invest in any business, but don't manage it, your profits are considered passive income, exactly what Webster was thinking about when he wrote the definition.

What about business? Well, that depends on how you set it up. Rich people create businesses and set up a system that the business follows. That way, if the owner goes on vacation for a month to Fiji, the employees follow the system and the owner still gets the profits. Any business will of course start out with a lot of work, but if you take the time to set up a business so that it gets reproducible results (exactly like a franchise), those profits become passive. And, according to the IRS, any salary you get from your business is considered "earned" but profits are considered "passive". It is vital when starting a business to check with an accountant and an attorney to set up your business that financially benefits you the best.

What else can be considered passive income? How about self-storage facilities, parking garages/lots and dry cleaners! They all require some time to start up, but once they are set up, you collect money over and over again.

Residual vs Passive Income

Residual and passive income are like siblings. They are both very similar and most people really consider them synonyms. What does it matter, anyway? They are both excellent ways to get money in your hands month after month after month without trading your time or your freedom. How can it get better than that?

Reality Check

Beware of anyone that tells you that there is NO work involved in passive income. Passive income does not mean no work! If you are going to invest in a business, a stock, or a real estate property, you will have to do your research (this is called "due diligence"). Research is work! You will also be required to manage your investments, to check up on their progress and make changes as necessary. That's work too!

The good news is that research and management is only a part-time endeavor. And most of the time, that work can be done from almost anywhere, including on a beach in Fiji.

Let us not forget the FUN factor. I'm sure there are some of you reading this who like, even love their jobs (if you still have one). Some of you have your own business - and congrats to you! But most of us are in jobs just because we need to feed our families and pay the bills. Looking into passive income streams and investing your time and money can bring you many, many returns. Researching for and implementing your passive income plans so that you can live your dreams is FUN. Getting money every month, week, or even every day is FUN. And trying out new strategies and managing your money - when you have some to manage - is FUN.

Passive income cash gotten from an action or source other than customary business or "work". Expressed another way, it isn't an aftereffect of exchanging "working time" for cash, for example, hourly, week after week or month to month compensation/ compensation. In this customary situation, on the off chance that you quit working, you quit being paid! In an automated revenue circumstance, you keep on accepting a pay stream notwithstanding when your are not effectively working. Three instances of winning passive income are:

1. You compose a book that keeps on selling quite a long time after year delivering an eminence stream.

2. You sell a protection arrangement that pays you a commission each month from that point.

3. You fabricate a site that sells numerous items, each speaking to a pay stream.

The following is a progressively complete rundown of potential wellsprings of automated revenue.

annuity installments

enthusiasm on ledgers or other money related instruments

sovereignties on a book

offers of a computerized/digital book

staggered showcasing pay plans

stock profit installments

rental pay from venture property

commissions from robotized rehash deals

offshoot commissions

educational cost from pre-bundled instruction programs

web based publicizing commissions

referral rewards

memberships or participations

candy machine item deals

Setting up Passive Income Streams

Since you have an essential comprehension of the this idea, you may research whether any of the previously mentioned passive income openings could work for you.

In checking on the rundown, an astonishing number of these wellsprings of automated revenue can be embraced for a sensible speculation of time and additionally cash. The five wellsprings of pay excerpted from the past rundown and appeared beneath may not be possible for you to seek after in light of the fact that they are essentially not accessible to you ie. annuity installments or they would necessitate that you as of now have a generous measure of money or other budgetary resources. Premium installments, stock profits, and speculation property are instances of the last mentioned. Be that as it may, the majority of the rest of the sources on the rundown might be pursuable alternatives relying upon your interests, aptitudes, experience, training, and so on. Absence of huge money saves or other fluid resources need not be obstructions to making salary streams from any at least one of these passive income openings.

As expressed over, the accompanying wellsprings of salary openings may not be accessible or promptly down to earth for you. Notwithstanding, as you start to amass increasingly money related riches, premium earned from budgetary records, stock profits and land speculations will move toward becoming alternatives for you to consider as automated revenue business openings.

annuity installments

Enthusiasm on ledgers or other money related instruments

stock profit installments

venture property pay

candy machine item deals

Your Legacy

One final advantage of setting up aloof surges of pay is that they can be passed on to your relatives, subsequently proceeding to upgrade your family's way of life. It is an all around acknowledged reason that passing on the methods for money age to your survivors is a vital aspect for structure "generational" riches.

You might think about what are approaches to profit on the web and how to get rich with types of easy revenue? Or then again regardless of whether there is a "simple automated revenue" to be made on the web?

Is it conceivable to get rich with types of automated revenue? Is that a genuine method to profit on the web? Numerous individuals may question that there is such an approach to achieve this when there are such a significant number of ways that can isolate you from your cash given every one of the tricks out there. This article will ideally impart to you a way or two of how to make passive income on the web.

You can profit on the web and even get rich with it since this is the main method for gaining cash that isn't attached to you changing your time for a fixed cash sum, or what is known as a check. Any type of automated revenue is, by definition, not attached to trading your time for cash. Not at all like a check which is actually just exchanging your time for cash, this type of salary of profiting on the web can enable you to get rich definitely on the grounds that this type of pay isn't attached to exchanging your time however depends on gaining cash over and over and in an inactive way which is gotten all the time.

Believe it or not, most of individuals online don't profit with their endeavors. They will never get rich with any type of profiting other than explicit types of non-straight salary that can be produced by and large with practically zero out of pocket costs to the person. Partner outlines to profit online that can - after some time - form into automated revenue and enable somebody to get rich are accessible from most subsidiary projects on the web. Building an online business and making a strong, standard pay is much of the time is the consequence of cautious research, showcase distinguishing proof, and legitimate and viable promoting procedures that produce deals and develop benefits. Most great partner projects have the online apparatuses, promotion duplicate and showcasing settings to enable associates to succeed and on the off chance that they put forth a concentrated effort to the errand of profiting on the web, they will succeed. Many, anyway observe the achievement of some offshoot advertisers and feel this is a simple automated revenue to be made, when the fact of the matter is a long way from it.

Subsidiaries who need to profit through their partner projects telecommuting can build up various surges of salary by following the outline spread out for them by the administrator of the program. People who recently worked for a check or a liner pay and afterward understanding that it would not enable them to get rich chose to begin an online business that could be worked to build up an passive incomestream and maybe more than one. The individuals who comprehend the idea of automated revenue rather than straight pay are attracted to the web to attempt to make their fantasies work out as expected through this medium.

Preceding going pedal to the metal into an online business and leaving their place of employment, numerous people intentionally choose to initially begin by working low maintenance to make a second pay that is an passive income instead of a second straight pay. Easy money scams must be kept away from no matter what as these are not genuine organizations, but instead past occasions to burn through one's time on the web.

Before considering prominent methods for producing an automated revenue online let us characterize what we mean by straight and easy revenue. Direct pay as we demonstrated above is a pay that is earned by exchanging your time for profiting, or working for another person. Basically, the more you work, the more you profit. Be that as it may, on the off chance that you don't work, you don't profit. That is the substance of a straight salary.

An easy revenue, be that as it may, is a type of profiting that is inactive in nature and does not require the exchanging of your opportunity to profit. An passive income will produce cash for you whether you work or not, accepting that you have found a way to create that pay in any case. When you have done that, your pay will be paid to you consistently and not on the grounds that you possess to exchange your energy for it, but since you are being paid for something that you have officially done, subsequently the automated revenue idea. Passive income can take numerous structures from land income, to venture profit to composing income, to singing profit [residuals] to profiting from your online endeavors. It can likewise get from system promoting, associate showcasing, and publicizing incomes from your online endeavors. For some individuals this is the thing that they allude to as profiting while they rest and view as simple easy revenue.

Just passive income will enable you to get rich. The more the automated revenue you make, the sooner you can get rich. Residuals, as certain individuals call this pay is the wellspring of every online fortune for the individuals who get rich on the web. When you are effective in setting up one online passive income stream it is simpler to do it a subsequent time, and after that a third, etc. Some express that the key to online achievement is to set up however many autonomous surges of passive income as could reasonably be expected so as to broaden and ensure one's advantage.

Things being what they are, would you like to make an passive income or a direct pay?

Exchanging your time for a check is minimal more than being a contracted slave. You work, you get paid. You don't work, you don't get paid. Straight salary is the term alluded to as the pay that keeps you poor. It has no effect whether you are a specialist, bank supervisor, a cab driver or a Walmart representative. The one basic component that these individuals offer is that they are exchanging their time for a check. In the event that they quit working, their compensation quits being paid.

Easy revenue, notwithstanding, is deliberately unique in that it is a salary that you get over and over for a move that you made beforehand however are never again doing. It is a salary that you will keep on getting regardless of whether you don't work any more. The more automated revenue streams you can set up the more salary you will make and the sooner you will get rich.

The best way to get rich online is to advance member programs that pay you abundantly and to set up a few of these that can profit online for you. Furthermore, recollect, when you have set up your enormous lucrative framework, you don't need to small scale oversee it to keep it running appropriately to create more associate pay for you. Really, a set it and overlook it framework is a definitive for effective online advertisers who direct their activities towards getting this sort of framework set up appropriately.

Straight versus automated revenue. The decision is clear, and the decision is yours. Work once and get paid once, or work once and get paid until the end of time. That is the mantra of offshoot advertisers wherever who comprehend the contrast among direct and automated revenue types of how to profit and they ceaselessly look for approaches to create salary streams that can fabricate their passive income after some time.

The direct salary stream is a type of drudgery that many feel they need to experience to gain a check. They make a cursory effort consistently, consistently, consistently, consistently, until, before they know it, their life has passed them by and they are griping about lost chances and how they passed up life.

Passive income streams, be that as it may, when they are set up and creating an:"easy pay" of an aloof sort are not drudgery. They are seen as paradise sent and are held up upon restlessly by the beneficiary. Automated revenue enables you to perform multiple tasks in that you can be accomplishing something different [like setting up another passive income stream] while you are getting this effectively settled one.

Or on the other hand, you can invest energy with your life partner, family, kids or companions doing what premium you, knowing very well indeed that your automated revenue stream is as yet creating a pay for you. A straight salary stream can't do that for you. In the event that you invest energy with family as opposed to working, you don't get paid. Straightforward as that.

A non-direct salary stream [or two] can give you your life back. Realizing that you will get it regardless of whether you quit doing what made it is solace and security. Why anybody would stop, in any case, is vague when you realize that by rehashing what you did in any case to create that pay you could do again to rehash the procedure to produce another different salary stream of an aloof sort.

On the off chance that you are capable, you should begin to produce your own flood of easy revenue. Do it low maintenance from the start and after that grow at your own pace. This isn't a medium-term get rich plan so it will require some investment to create. On the off chance that it takes both of you or three or even five years to complete it right, what does it make a difference to you? However, in the event that you don't begin to create this sort of salary you will perpetually be obligated to a direct kind of pay that must be accessible as long as you keep on working. When you stop, that salary stops. An automated revenue, in any case, will keep on being dropped into your financial balance notwithstanding when you at long last "resign".

One of the keys to getting rich and making riches is to comprehend the various manners by which pay can be produced. It's frequently said that the lower and white collar class work for cash while the rich have cash work for them. The way to riches creation exists in this basic explanation.

Envision, as opposed to you working for cash that you rather made each dollar work for you 40hrs every week. Even better, envision every single dollar working for you day in and day out for example 168hrs/week. Making sense of the most ideal ways you can make cash work for you is a significant advance headed straight toward riches creation.

In the US, the Internal Revenue Service (IRS) government organization in charge of duty gathering and authorization, classifies salary into three wide types: dynamic (earned) pay, easy revenue, and portfolio pay. Any cash you ever make (other than possibly winning the lottery or accepting a legacy) will can be categorized as one of these pay classes. So as to see how to end up rich and make riches it's essential that you realize how to create numerous surges of automated revenue.

Intersection the Chasm

Automated revenue is salary produced from an exchange or business, which does not require the worker to take an interest. It is regularly venture salary (for example salary that isn't gotten through working) yet not only. The focal precept of this kind of pay is that it can hope to proceed with whether you keep working or not. As you close to retirement you are without a doubt looking to supplant earned pay with detached, unmerited pay. The key to riches creation prior on in life is automated revenue; positive income produced by resources that you control or possess.

One reason individuals think that its hard to make the jump from earned salary to progressively aloof wellsprings of pay is that the whole instruction framework is in reality essentially intended to instruct us to carry out a responsibility and henceforth depend generally on earned pay. This works for governments as this sort of salary produces enormous volumes of assessment yet won't work for you in case you're spotlight is on the most proficient method to end up rich and riches building. Be that as it may, to end up rich and make riches you will be required to cross the gorge from depending on earned pay as it were.

Land and Business - Sources of Passive Income

The aloof kind of salary isn't reliant on your time. It is subject to the advantage and the administration of that benefit. Automated revenue requires utilizing of different people groups time and cash. For instance, you could buy an investment property for $100,000 utilizing a 30% initial installment and acquire 70% from the bank. Accepting this property creates a 6% Net Yield (Gross Yield short all Operational Costs, for example, protection, support, property charges, the executives expenses and so on) you would produce a net rental yield of $6,000/annum or $500/month. Presently, subtract the expense of the home loan reimbursements of state $300/month from this and we land at a net rental pay of $200 from this. This is $200 passive income you didn't possess to exchange your energy for.

Business can be a wellspring of automated revenue. Numerous business visionaries begin in business with beginning a business to sell their stake for somewhere in the range of millions in state 5 years time. This fantasy will possibly turn into a reality in the event that you, the business visionary, can make yourself replaceable with the goal that the business' future salary age isn't subject to you. In the event that you can do this than in a manner you have made a wellspring of easy revenue. For a business, to turn into a genuine wellspring of automated revenue it requires the correct sort of frameworks and the correct sort of individuals (other than you) working those frameworks.

At last, since passive income producing resources are normally effectively constrained by you the proprietor (for example an investment property or a business), you have a state in the everyday tasks of the benefit which can decidedly affect the degree of pay produced.

Automated revenue - A Misnomer?

Somehow or another, automated revenue is a misnomer as there is nothing really aloof about being in charge of a gathering of benefits creating pay. Regardless of whether it's a property portfolio or a business you claim and control, it is only very seldom really inactive. It will expect you to be required at some level in the administration of the benefit. Nonetheless, it's uninvolved as in it doesn't require your everyday direct inclusion (or if nothing else it shouldn't in any case!)

To end up rich, consider building utilized/automated revenue by developing the size and level of your system rather than essentially developing your abilities/skill. Purported brilliant people may invest their energy gathering confirmations and testaments however well off society invest their time gathering business cards and building connections!

Leftover Income = A Form of Passive Income

Leftover Income is a type of automated revenue. The terms Passive Income and Residual Income are regularly utilized reciprocally; notwithstanding, there is an unpretentious yet significant contrast between the two. It is pay that is produced every once in a while from work done once for example repeating installments that you get long after the underlying item/deal is made. Lingering salary is as a rule in explicit sums and paid at customary interims. Some case of remaining pay incorporate:-

- Royalties/profit from the distributing of a book.

- Renewal commissions on money related items paid to a budgetary guide.

- Rentals from a property letting.

- Revenue created in staggered showcasing systems.

Utilization of Other People's Resources and Other People's Money

Utilization of Other People's Resources and Other People's Money are key fixing required to produce automated revenue. Other People's Money gets you time (a key restricting component of earned salary in riches creation). As it were, utilization of other individuals' assets gives you back your time. With regards to raising capital, organizations that produce passive income for the most part pulls in the biggest measure of Other People's Money. This is on the grounds that it is commonly conceivable to firmly inexact the arrival (or if nothing else the hazard) you can anticipate from uninvolved ventures thus banks and so on., will frequently subsidize detached speculation openings. A decent field-tested strategy upheld by solid administration will typically draw in heavenly attendant financial specialists or funding cash. Also, land can regularly be procured with a little up front installment (20% or less now and again) with most of the cash acquired from a bank ordinarily.

Tax breaks of Passive Income

Automated revenue ventures frequently take into account the most ideal expense treatment whenever organized accurately. For instance, enterprises can utilize their benefits to put resources into other aloof speculations (land, for instance), and profit of duty reasonings all the while. Also, land can be "exchanged" for bigger land, with duties conceded inconclusively. The expense paid on passive income will shift dependent on the person's close to home duty section and corporate structures used. In any case, for the motivations behind outline we could state that a normal of 20% successful expense on aloof speculations would be a sensible presumption.

In light of current circumstances, passive income is regularly viewed as the sacred goal of contributing, and the way to long haul riches creation and riches security. The real advantage of passive income is that it is repeating salary, ordinarily created quite a long time after month without a lot of exertion by you. Building riches and getting to be rich shouldn't be tied in with extricating each and every piece of your own vitality, your own assets and your own cash as there is constantly a point of confinement to the degree you can do this. Taking advantage of the viable age and utilization of passive income is a basic advance making progress toward riches creation. Start this piece of you riches creation venture as right on time as is humanly conceivable for example presently!

On the off chance that you scan the web for "easy revenue", you may discover a definition or two, however for the most part, what you find are sites attempting to sell you on the automated revenue kind of-the-day. It's disappointing, I know. I don't think about you, yet before I bounce into any chance or even before I travel, I like to do my exploration. That being stated, there are a ton of good open doors out there. Be that as it may, before you start burning through cash, we should examine what passive income is and, in particular, what it isn't.

Webster's word reference characterizes automated revenue as "of, identifying with, or being business movement in which the speculator does not have quick command over salary". I don't believe that recounts to the entire story. Passive income is cash that you get again and again without doing much work (see I didn't state "any work"). It is not quite the same as earned salary in that you are not getting cash for your time (like you would work). However, contingent upon the automated revenue stream that you pick, you may in reality have quick command over your salary. However, I'll get to that later.

For what reason would you need automated revenue? All things considered, similar to Robert Kiyosaki clarifies in his book Rich Dad Poor Dad, that is the principle distinction between the rich and the white collar class. The rich put their cash in different automated revenue streams. At the point when their passive income surpasses their costs, at that point they are monetarily free. "Monetarily free" essentially implies that you don't must have a normal everyday employment to pay your costs. Furthermore, you are "free" to then do anything you desire!

What Passive Income Isn't

Before I go into revealing to you what passive income is, let me first disclose to you need it isn't. Automated revenue isn't a similar thing as "leftover salary". Remaining pay is cash that you get all the time in the wake of having done work once. The best model would be TV sitcoms. A few entertainers get "residuals". On-screen characters get paid for taping the show. A while later, a few entertainers get paid each time the show rehashes. Salesmen that sell administrations, memberships, or sustainable items (like protection) sell that thing once and, giving the client restores, will get a commission off of every reestablishment. Eminences from the closeout of books and music are additionally leftover.

Many state that staggered promoting or system advertising deals furnish you with automated revenue. Prepare to be blown away. That is lingering as well.

On the off chance that you have a private company or are independently employed, regardless of whether you are profiting, this isn't automated revenue. On the off chance that you get a compensation from your business, that is earned pay. There is an approach to transform this into easy revenue, be that as it may - so stay tuned.

You know, I need to state that beginning your very own site can't be easy revenue. Regardless of whether you are selling an item, (for example, an eBook, course or other data) or an administration, despite everything you need to showcase your site. You should do this paying little mind to whether you are selling your OWN items or reserve the privileges to sell other's items. Showcasing your site is work, straightforward as that. In any case, it is anything but a vocation. Furthermore, when your promoting endeavors start taking off, you can profit with minimal extra exertion. In any case, that is remaining in my book, not latent.

What Passive Income IS

Passive income is a great deal of things. The principal thing that rings a bell, and furthermore, I accept, the most mainstream model is land. On the off chance that you claim venture property and are getting a positive income from a house, business property, or loft, that is easy revenue. On the off chance that you lease rooms in your home, that is automated revenue as well. You just need to set this up once, and afterward the pay comes in a seemingly endless amount of time after month. Premium pay from investment accounts, CDs, and currency market records are latent - the bank pays you for keeping your cash in those records. On the off chance that you have a site with standard advertisements or Google AdSense promotions, that can be called latent also.

On the off chance that you put resources into any business, however don't oversee it, your benefits are viewed as easy revenue, precisely what Webster was pondering when he composed the definition.

Shouldn't something be said about business? Indeed, that relies upon how you set it up. Rich individuals make organizations and set up a framework that the business pursues. That way, if the proprietor travels for a month to Fiji, the representatives pursue the framework and the proprietor still gets the benefits. Any business will obviously begin with a ton of work, however in the event that you set aside the effort to set up a business so it gets reproducible outcomes (precisely like an establishment), those benefits become uninvolved. What's more, as per the IRS, any pay you get from your business is considered "earned" however benefits are considered "uninvolved". It is crucial when beginning a business to check with a bookkeeper and a lawyer to set up your business that monetarily benefits you the best.

What else can be viewed as easy revenue? What about self-storerooms, parking structures/parts and cleaners! They all require some an opportunity to fire up, however once they are set up, you gather cash again and again.

Remaining versus Passive Income

Remaining and automated revenue resemble kin. They are both fundamentally the same as and the vast majority truly think about them equivalent words. What does it make a difference, in any case? They are both brilliant approaches to get cash in your grasp quite a long time after a seemingly endless amount of time after month without exchanging your time or your opportunity. How might it improve than that?

Rude awakening

Be careful with anybody that reveals to you that there is NO work engaged with easy revenue. Passive income does not mean no work! On the off chance that you will put resources into a business, a stock, or a land property, you should do your examination (this is designated "due perseverance"). Research is work! You will likewise be required to deal with your speculations, to determine the status of their advancement and make changes as important. That is work as well!

Fortunately research and the board is just low maintenance try. What's more, more often than not, that work should be possible from anyplace, incorporating on a shoreline in Fiji.

Let us not overlook the FUN factor. I'm certain there are some of you perusing this who like, even love their employments (on the off chance that despite everything you have one). Some of you have your own business - and well done to you! However, the majority of us are in employments since we have to sustain our families and cover the tabs. Investigating passive income streams and contributing your time and cash can bring you many, numerous profits. Inquiring about for and executing your automated revenue designs with the goal that you can live your fantasies is FUN. Getting cash each month, week, or even each day is FUN. What's more, evaluating new systems and dealing with your cash - when you have some to oversee - is FUN.

I expectation I've carried out my responsibility and given you the passive income nuts and bolts. In the event that you have any inquiries or considerations, don't hesitate to get in touch with me through my site. I'd love to get notification from you!

The most effective method to Generate Passive
Income

The vast majority concur that the way to progress is
constancy. They are reluctant to get behind the race.
These proactive individuals have demonstrated to
wind up stable in their life. Then again, the languid
don't have any issue essentially in light of the fact that
they don't have anything too. The two kinds of
individuals have been so. It sounds reasonable, isn't
that right?

Be that as it may, this balance is the relic of times
gone by. On the off chance that this is our outlook,
we will without a doubt be astounded at the
extraordinary fortune of the individuals who have
applied less exertion and at the dissatisfaction of the
individuals who have put forth a valiant effort. It
doesn't imply that life is uncalled for. Actually, we
acquire from what we do as well as from what we
don't do. The previous is known as dynamic pay; the
last mentioned, inactive.

Dynamic salary is a pay we create from our diligent
work. When we work for cash, it is dynamic salary. In
any case, when it is our very own cash that works for
us, it is automated revenue. Passive income is a salary
we produce from our venture. Step by step
instructions to produce automated revenue without

dynamic intercession is certifiably not a sort of enchantment that everybody could have.

How to create easy revenue? Passive income is created when our speculation acquires due to our convenient choice. In this kind of salary, we are paid for the choice we make and for the hazard we take. When we become scared of contributing, we tend not to settle on any choice. Thusly, nothing happens to our cash. To produce automated revenue, we should settle on the correct choice on what and when to contribute and not choose about not contributing. We should likewise ascertain the hazard - the higher the hazard, the higher the arrival. The lower the hazard implies the more it takes to get the potential return. It relies upon what our identity is and what venture accommodates our character. Proactive individuals are normally profession arranged so they can effectively produce dynamic pay. Then again, understanding individuals are savvy leaders and daring people.

Presently, the inquiry is which sort of workers we ought to be. Dynamic workers have full control of the amount they could gain, however there is limit in the sum as there is limit in their vitality and time. When they stop, so does their pay. Notwithstanding, uninvolved workers are progressively effective as in they appreciate the boundless capability of procuring high with less vitality. Besides, uninvolved workers can be both dynamic and inactive workers. Clearly, passive income is increasingly worthwhile.

It isn't hard to tell how to create automated revenue. There is a great deal of accessible data around us that can enable us to figure out how to start this with. We for the most part have found out about contributing and among the well known are securities exchange, securities, common assets, protection, annuity plans, and treasury notes. Prior to contributing, it is essential to contemplate your decision venture. We don't need to be the handyman. What is significant is that we comprehend the hazard and the capability of the market we need to enter and begin little only for an attempt. As time passes by, we will pick up understanding and will ace the market we have picked. In the approach of innovation, it has turned out to be simpler to get more data about any field of undertaking. The web offers various apparatuses we have to end up prepared.

The most essential piece of how to produce passive income is our frame of mind toward venture. A few people believe that venture is done so as to continue our day by day need and this is an off-base thought. Provided that this is true, it isn't any greater venture. It is business. Our quick need must be supported by dynamic salary. To rely upon speculation for every day needs is flighty. We should work so as to live and we contribute in light of the fact that we secure our tomorrow. Genuine financial specialists are future situated. They don't actually make cash immediately. In any case, their cash makes them. That is the motivation behind why we call this condition detached. Everyone's need today is not the same as our need later on. Our prompt need is replied by our quick activity and prompt outcomes cause us to develop. In any case, passive income isn't something that should cause us to develop. This is something that we ought to develop. In this way, whatever we procure now is the thing that we need now. Dynamic salary is the impression of we do now. The correct frame of mind toward automated revenue is to regard it as a different living element. Dynamic salary is the thing that we need now. Also, passive income is the thing that our venture need now. It resembles a pet that we should raise.

Shouldn't something be said about business? Is it a sort of dynamic pay or detached? As a matter of fact, it is the blend of both. A representative effectively controls his money streams to continue his day by day needs and simultaneously save some greater part for his business as a different element. Be that as it may, organizations are perplexing these days relying upon their size. Enormous partnerships are for the most part possessed by various individuals called investors. They enlist administrators and even CEO's to effectively control their tasks. Now and again, they intercede in a large scale level. However, their control and exertion are constrained contrasted with the noteworthy pay they get each year if their organizations constantly develop.

For these individuals, these enormous organizations are their wellspring of automated revenue. For little businesspeople, they should apply all their exertion for their business. They experience difficulty causing their organizations to develop on the grounds that they additionally rely upon the dynamic salary they create from working their organizations. Would this imply so as to create easy revenue, we ought to have had huge funding to contribute? Not really! We can do as such by putting resources into portions of stocks even in littler measure of cash. This is likewise valid with shared supports that pool singular interests in modest quantity to make it one major speculation. This implies we produce passive income like huge speculators.

At the time, I didn't have a great deal of cash. In any case, everybody needs to begin some place, isn't that so? My first involvement in this domain, other than enthusiasm on my bank account, was purchasing a sweet machine, filling it with M&Ms and setting it in the parlor at my fencing club. I determined the expense of a solitary M&M and made sense of what number of M&Ms I would give different fencers for their 25 pennies. Since I at that point knew my overall revenue per deal, I found that I was making a normal $25 every month in passive income subsequent to giving 10% back to the lesser fencing program.

A few people think they are accepting automated revenue when they are really getting leftover salary.

For instance, a protection specialist may win lingering pay as her customers restore their protection approaches. In any case, if the protection operator leaves the organization, that pay leaves.

In case you're associated with a systems administration showcasing or staggered promoting organization in which you need to keep on working the business so as to get salary, that is false automated revenue either. On the off chance that you can quit working the business all together for whatever length of time that you need and still keep on gaining pay, that is easy revenue.

The enormous legend about automated revenue is that once you purchase or make a benefit that produces it for you, you're finished. You might be under the feeling that you don't need to invest any more energy in it or oversee it.

In all actuality there are differing degrees of "inactive." For instance, you can get automated revenue from rental land, yet land can be amazingly tedious. Normally, when you purchase a property, there is an underlying adjustment process that can incorporate anything from doing fixes to finding and screening new inhabitants. When the property is balanced out, you might most likely kick back and simply get lease checks for some time, yet then an occupant moves out, or the water radiator breaks or a tree falls on the rooftop, and you need to invest energy in the property once more.

That is altogether different from an authentication of store at the bank where you get it, and that is it. Obviously, your potential pay on the investment property is a lot higher than the potential salary on the endorsement of store in the event that you realize what you're doing.

Be aware of the distinction among latent and leftover pay, and of how precisely how "inactive" a speculation truly is.

For what reason is automated revenue significant?

Suppose you didn't need to rely upon a vocation, a companion, your family, the legislature or any other individual for cash. That is the thing that this sort of pay can accommodate you.

In numerous customary monetary arranging models, you're urged to make sense of how a lot of cash you'll require when you need to resign. Upon retirement, you spend that cash. This arrangement has some genuine imperfections. Above all else, imagine a scenario in which you live longer than you expect and outlast your cash. Second of all, consider the possibility that in the wake of placing in such a great amount of vitality to set aside that cash, you would want to leave it as an inheritance as opposed to spending it.

The way to money related autonomy is this:

$$PI > E$$

At the point when your automated revenue (PI) is more noteworthy than your costs (E), you are in finished decision about what you do with your time in light of the fact that your advantages will keep on paying for your way of life whether you work or not.

In all actuality to be monetarily autonomous, you don't should be sans obligation, pay off your home, profit or be a mogul. You simply must have more pay than costs.

It's that straightforward.

Passive income enables you to have MORE CHOICES. You can live out of delight and opportunity rather than obligation and commitment.

On an increasingly genuine note, imagine a scenario where something awful occurred and you couldn't work any longer. How might you take care of your tabs? When you have enough automated revenue, you additionally have more significant serenity.

There are two sections to this equation. To turn out to be monetarily free quicker, you can expand your automated revenue, and you can likewise inspect how to diminish your costs.

So how would you get progressively easy revenue?

There are two principle sorts of easy revenue. The primary sort is detached speculation pay. So as to get latent speculation pay, you need subsidizes accessible to put resources into these pay vehicles. In the event that you have reserves accessible to contribute, you have to concentrate on doing a fitting measure of research and due ingenuity to choose which of these uninvolved vehicles are best for your circumstance and hazard resilience.

The subsequent sort originates from making your very own pay vehicle with next to zero cash. For instance, you may begin a site that produces income from promotions or join a system advertising organization that will enable you to keep on getting salary when you are never again effectively working the business. Or on the other hand you may go into business or become a subsidiary of another person's the same old thing.

On the off chance that you have cash to contribute, you will most likely have the option to create salary more rapidly than somebody who doesn't. In the event that you don't have any cash to contribute, you must be happy to contribute time, vitality, aptitudes, assets, imagination or these.

As far as I can tell, the most practical approach to manufacture automated revenue is to concentrate on steady development. Start by making one little stride. Try not to attempt to create an extra $10,000 every month in automated revenue right this moment. Concentrate on what you can do to produce $10 every month in automated revenue and go from that point.

In the event that you are looking for an automated revenue opportunity you are certainly destined for success towards making monetary opportunity. Passive income is what is regularly alluded to as brilliant cash and it is the favored strategy with which the rich win their pay. Automated revenue is salary that keeps on being produced long after the underlying exertion or work. You actually get paid again and again for work done once.

Most of individuals acquire their living through straight salary which is pay that is legitimately relative to the time and exertion you put in. Automated revenue gives you money related opportunity, yet more significantly it gives you the opportunity of time. With automated revenue you will acquire cash paying little mind to whether you work or not. I constantly preferred the similarity of an apple tree. When you've planted it and it developed it will continue proving to be fruitful season after season. Making automated revenue streams for yourself resembles planting little apple trees. When they developed they will continue proving to be fruitful and as they become greater and more grounded throughout the years they will create much more and better natural product.

In spite of the fact that this idea sounds inconceivably appealing, the test as normal seems to be 'the manner by which?' Passive pay has turned into somewhat of a catchphrase and Robert Kiyosaki's Rich Dad books truly promoted the term. It will in general be a bit of deluding as the word 'detached' will in general be mistaken for 'programmed' or sitting idle. Despite the fact that the passive incomeis uninvolved, regardless you need to set it up and plant the apple tree. Automated revenue won't be given to you with a royal flair. On the off chance that it's produced through property, at that point despite everything you need to discover it, make the arrangement, get it and do all the desk work and administrator included. On the off chance that you wish to win automated revenue by composing a book, or a play or a motion picture, regardless you need to plunk down, compose it, distribute it and experience all the different customs before you can kick back and appreciate the opportunity of uninvolved repeating pay.

Today there are more passive income openings than any time in recent memory, both on the web and disconnected. The web most importantly has opened up an immense new world with various roads to investigate in for all intents and purposes any specialty showcase you can consider. Detecting a great passive income opportunity can be somewhat of a test as the sheer measure of decisions can be overpowering.

There are fundamentally two different ways of procuring passive income on the web (in spite of the fact that it's not only a web based thing). The first is to make your very own item or thought and to offer it to another person who will do the promoting and 'selling' for you. You would then gain eminences for this. Acquiring eminences is extremely basic in the music business and can be profoundly rewarding. Be that as it may, in the event that you don't the following number one hit single in you head, at that point there is an extremely ground-breaking elective.

You don't have to make your own item to gain automated revenue. You can win passive income off other individuals' items through partner and partner programs. You can assemble a site, where you take the necessary steps once, however win repeating salary through partner commissions. This is just one of numerous ways you can acquire automated revenue on the web. It appears as though the greatest test isn't in finding an automated revenue opportunity, yet rather in choosing one. Here are some fundamental rules to enable you to recognize a decent passive income opportunity.

Be cautious about over-expanded tributes and guarantees. The majority of them are made up. Attempt and cross check the different tributes and check' whether you can coordinate what they guarantee. On the off chance that you can contact the individual giving the tribute, at that point do as such. There is in no way like genuine answers and counsel from somebody who is really making a triumph from what you are going to set out on.

» Do your due determination on the organization that drives the program. With regards to member programs, remain with the 'serious canons resembles

Clickbank, Commission Junction and Linkshare (there are a lot increasingly solid ones out there) beyond what many would consider possible. They are more averse to vanish following 2 years and there is nothing more regrettable than buckling down to set up your passive income framework just to see it dissipate like a phantom.

» There are a lot of automated revenue openings in 'prevailing fashion' and 'hot' items, yet they once in a while keep going long haul. You may do well for two or three months, yet that scarcely legitimizes the underlying work and the possibility of gaining lifetime commission that you could procure. Ensure than when you do advance items that they have a not too bad lifetime and utilize your own trustworthiness. Attempt and think two years ahead and check whether the item will at present be required and whether it has potential for development.

» Make sure that you accept and trust in the item. On the off chance that you don't, at that point you could always be unable to advance it with the important certainty should have been effective. Setting up an passive income framework requires an incredible beginning push and it very well may be difficult to get it going. Ensure it's something you cherish, something you have confidence in and something worth while. This is essential in making the vital inspiration.

An passive income open door is just that - a chance. Until and except if you snatch it and make a move it will do nothing for you. It's never extremely about the chance, yet rather about what you do with the open door that truly tallies. You have nothing to free and everything to pick up. Keep in mind that we just will in general lament the things we don't do. The one thing I know beyond a shadow of a doubt is this: passive income truly make me rest very well around evening time!

These days, it is hard to discover wellsprings of pay. The hole between the rich and the poor is augmenting. Some state that in the event that you buckle down, you will consistently have salary to endure. Be that as it may, what will you do in the event that it is extremely elusive a vocation? In reality, even the rich think that its difficult to keep their pay. In any case, this is to a lesser extent an issue for some who realize where to discover wellsprings of automated revenue.

In this way, let us characterize automated revenue first. Passive income is a sort of pay earned from venture. There are two kinds of salary - dynamic and inactive. We gain dynamic salary from the aftereffect of our work. Pay rates, commissions, and administration expenses are wellsprings of dynamic pay. What are the wellsprings of easy revenue? Wellsprings of pay have various structures. Some famous sources are: profits, premium earned, lease, deals, land, gear, and cash itself.

Profit

Profit is earned from the net benefit of an organization. It is a type of benefit sharing and it is increasingly normal in securities exchange. At the point when an organization is claimed by a few people or more, the benefit is partitioned in extent to every proprietor's venture. These proprietors are called investors and such a benefit is known as profit. Profit can be money or stock. It is a money profit when the benefit is dispersed in real money through bank checks. What's more, it is a stock profit when it is conveyed as offers or stock. As one of the wellsprings of automated revenue, profit is likewise alluring particularly during the time of development. Not all organizations give reliable profits. Remember that stock choice decides your future salary. In the event that the organization chose is demonstrated to give higher profits, there will be a major plausibility that it will proceed. Most organizations that reliably give higher profits are called pay stocks. Salary stocks may not be enormous organizations. Truth be told, even some enormous organizations miss the mark in making reliable profits because of their surprising expense of activity. In this way, not all stocks are certain wagered as one of the wellsprings of automated revenue.

Among the numerous wellsprings of salary in the securities exchange is a "pay stock" which is subject to their great industry condition. For example, if the IT business is alluring, any IT organization can be an up-and-comer as a wellspring of automated revenue. This implies it is smarter to look over those organizations than to pick a huge organization of which the business has been experiencing financial unrest. In this manner, a great wellspring of passive income in financial exchange is an organization from a decent industry.

Premium Earned

Premium earned is additionally noticeable as one of the wellsprings of easy revenue. When we store our cash in a bank, our cash gains loan cost. What is financing cost? Financing cost is the rate charged when we acquire some cash and it is earned when we loan. Despite the fact that we are not really a moneylender, we can likewise acquire this in light of the fact that our cash that we have kept in a bank adds to the sum that the bank has loaned to borrowers. Obviously, there is a condition before we think about our stores as wellsprings of salary.

We can believe our reserve funds to be one a wellspring of automated revenue. This possibly happens when the loan cost is high and our store is in critical sum. Time store or bank bonds are instances of uninvolved salaries. Investment account, as well, can be one. Banks vary from each other in loan fees. In this way, to get an appealing pay through the banks, we ought to pick the correct bank and store at the ideal time when the financing cost is high.

Lease and Lease

Wellsprings of passive income are various and complex, yet the most straightforward one is through lease or rent. Everyone knows with no clarification that pay we get from having our property leased or rented has demonstrated to give us dependable wellspring of salary. In the event that you have an additional house and parcel or a unit of condo, you will just need to get someone willing to involve the spot. Your wellsprings of automated revenue here isn't really your property however a solid occupant who can pay the lease reliably and can remain longer. The main thought here is the profile of your inhabitant. On the off chance that your property is a business parcel, you may have it rented to those specialists setting up a café, a service station, or a stockroom. The profile of your inhabitant here is more solid than the family ones. Business parcel occupants will definitely remain longer. This can really turn into your worry since this kind of speculation isn't fluid. It is a long haul speculation. All things considered, huge numbers of us will think about this as a standout amongst other wellspring of pay.

Interest in transportation administration anyway is not really viewed as one of the potential sources. The hazard required here is high. In any case, in the event that you are only a standard person who claims a couple of units of taxi, it is great to lease them out gave that you put a little in your vehicles' deterioration.

Deals

Purchase and-sell business can be a few wellsprings of pay contingent upon the things or products you exchange. The greater the things you exchange, the more latent the salary progresses toward becoming. On the off chance that we exchange littler things, that is promoting and a decent wellspring of dynamic salary. Be that as it may, if what we purchase and sell are vehicles, house and parcels, stocks, and bonds, they are certainly extraordinary wellsprings of easy revenue.

Land

Land is the best wellspring of salary. It doesn't need to be from leasing it out. Since days of yore, it has been the most dependable wellspring of pay. Before, rich land could deliver crops, trees, plants and grains without human mediation. Indeed, even animals and poultry were results of ripe land. Every one of these things that land could create were wellsprings of automated revenue. Such conditions are still valid as of not long ago, yet with little intercession.

Gear

In the nation, gear has turned out to be one of the wellsprings of automated revenue. Rice factory is the most prominent gear that you can live off in the homestead. During harvest season, ranchers line their sacks of rice to a processing station. A rice factory proprietor will gain a specific sum for each sack. After gather season, the income of rice factory proprietors is significantly more advantageous than that of the ranchers. During this post reap season, rice plant is not really fundamental. Be that as it may, some different harvests and grains are sought after of different sorts of hardware. For peanuts, shelling machines and graders are in front. Different sorts of hardware in the homestead are ranch tractors, processors, and dryers.

Indeed, even in the city, gear is one of the great wellsprings of easy revenue. Substantial gear utilized in development can be leased to temporary workers and engineers. In the event that you are a normal individual, you can secure a candy machine. A candy machine is being leased. You will really acquire from your sold items. In any case, it is viewed as an automated revenue since it is your machine that works for you. The most well known and the most vigorously leased hardware found in the city is the printing press. This is a business and simultaneously a speculation.

A normal individual can create automated revenue from various perspectives. This implies it isn't just the rich that can produce easy revenue. Everyone can except not similarly. For a normal individual, his pay is the main wellspring of pay he can produce. Past his insight, it is additionally conceivable to get some additional salary even without attempting to begin enormous.

Our compensation is valuable to us. Yet, beside our compensation we can gain a better than average sum from what minimal expenditure we have. The principal thing we ought to do is to set aside cash. Setting aside cash requires discipline. Around us, there are numerous things that power us to purchase what is past our prompt need. We should concur that to produce automated revenue, we need enough capital. We are simply confounded how nothing more will be tolerated. At whatever point our pay builds, we will in general spend more, as well. This is the greatest test to produce automated revenue.

We don't really spare all our well deserved cash to raise the required money to contribute. What we need is to ascertain the expense of our every day necessities and recognize the needs. As a rule, we organize which we ought to spend for. To create automated revenue has been overlooked by numerous individuals as the primary thing as a main priority. On the off chance that we put aside a little every time we get our compensation, such cash will turn out to be huge after some time. It is actually quite difficult. Notwithstanding, that is definitely not a hard activity. Our first need must be to produce automated revenue.

More often than not, we accept that solitary a major capital can produce automated revenue and it is past our farthest point. Maybe, it is valid. It is valid in the event that we keep on accepting so. Nowadays, the sky is the limit. Quite a while prior, we needed to get ready huge measure of capital on the grounds that the required least capital for practically a wide range of speculation was additionally huge. These days, the web offers numerous choices to create automated revenue.

In securities exchange, we can begin exchanging on the off chance that we have in any event $2,000 or even less. On the off chance that you put resources into financial exchange for a little measure of cash, the profit won't be much alluring regardless of how great the organization is. Nonetheless, you can produce automated revenue through purchasing and selling of stocks. There is hazard associated with exchanging stocks. In any case, in the event that you know about the fundamental devices on the most proficient method to deal with the hazard, financial exchange will be especially energizing and promising.

In the event that you are a traditionalist kind of financial specialists with little measure of cash and who are eager to hang tight for long, you may pick an oversaw portfolio, for example, the shared reserve. In common finance, you can place your cash in and haul out whenever you like. The base capital isn't huge, either. Your cash contributed is pooled together with the cash contributed by numerous individual financial specialists. This cash is the reserve being utilized to put resources into various arrangement of venture. You may produce passive income here through stock valuation and through stock profits of the store's portfolios. At the point when the store develops, you cash will, as well.

Presently, on the off chance that you are a daring person who needs to exploit the benefit capability of an unpredictable market, you may likewise exchange monetary forms for as meager as $500 or even less. To create automated revenue here, you should be a convey broker kind of financial specialists who conjecture a long haul bull pattern and acquire from a money's move over rate while making the most of your value edge or coasting benefit. Be that as it may, this is just valid in an awesome economic situation. In this sort of venture, just 5% or so of the individuals who attempt become proficient dealers. It doesn't imply that it is difficult to acquire here. Truth be told, money exchanging has the most astounding benefit potential because of high influence. What really this market requires is a profound comprehension of the hidden major and specialized motivation behind why a specific cash moves a single way. At the end of the day, aptitudes are required here. Then again, this is the least expensive approach to create automated revenue. It is additionally the most fluid market you may put resources into. Be that as it may, this is minimal detached of a wide range of automated revenue. Speculation here is neither subject to the market, nor on a money. It relies upon you and what sort of broker you are. In the event that you create passive income here, you should attempt a demo account first so as to test your exchanging methodology before contributing live account.

Notwithstanding, there are as yet huge numbers of us who resort to the customary method to create automated revenue. One can set up a sustenance truck business, or purchase a vehicle to make it a taxi. On the off chance that you officially possess a little unit of condo, you can have it leased. You may acquire some less expensive games hardware and set up a rec center in your locale. Business is by a long shot the most prevalent wellspring of salary. The issue is that the vast majority attempt the equivalent. In this way, rivalry gets considerably harder.

A sustenance truck business can be an exceptionally rewarding choice to produce easy revenue. Inside the shopping centers, a great deal of sustenance trucks line up. One may imagine that such a business isn't changeless. Shockingly, these little trucks have been developing in numbers. To work such a business isn't generally troublesome. Since it is little, the activity is basic and the expense is less. Be that as it may, it sells like hot cake.

Working a taxi is as simple as ABC. The perfect condition in this is the point at which the taxi unit is 100% claimed by you. This elective wellspring of salary is appropriate for the individuals who as of now have in any event one eco-friendly vehicle.

A normal individual who has acquired a little house and part or a loft unit may lease it out to create easy revenue. The returns from leasing your loft can be utilized to pay another lodging credit. Such a framework is for a long haul venture. Utilizing our properties to produce passive income for longer venture is an insightful choice we can make. Utilizing them to procure a living can be brief in light of the fact that our property deteriorates extra time. In spite of the fact that the estimation of land is acknowledging, auxiliary support is expensive. Beside that, inhabitants may go back and forth. Along these lines, you must be increasingly imaginative in using your assets.

You can likewise change over your property to a wellness rec center. Sports hardware devalues gradually. These days, numerous individuals are obsessed with wellbeing and wellness. There is a major market for that and this industry has been developing reliably. As our general public turns out to be increasingly unpleasant, individuals give increasingly more accentuation on adapting up pressure. Such a developing interest is a decent chance to produce automated revenue. While your clients pay for the vitality they devour, you are paid for the less exertion you apply.

Presently, there is additionally an option in contrast to conventional business. This business is known as online business. You may make and sell computerized items. Every single such exchange are presently done on the web. There are wide assortments of online organizations you can look over. What online business requires is your imagination. Everyone here is doing everything to drive the traffic to their locales and that will compel us to consider better systems. Despite the fact that the challenge is intense, the space for development is huge. What is significant is that you can begin here whenever with less capital and less chance.

Openings come in numerous structures. Some state that open door thumps just once. Others state it just waits. Whichever is genuine is anything but a major ordeal. It is the means by which one gets the chance. A great many people would concur that a pay opportunity is the best open door they could have. This is the motivation behind why everyone searches for it. All things considered, some could scarcely discover it. To truly get the open door does not really involve much vitality. One great similarity is the lion. Lions get their prey after ten endeavors. When they eat their unfortunate casualties, they will have utilized all their vitality. In this way, their dinner is only enough to supplant their lost vitality and that vitality is additionally only enough for one more day to get another prey. Despite what might be expected, crocodiles simply drift on the water and hang tight for their prey and they never let it pass. After their supper, they will be full and won't get ravenous notwithstanding for quite a while without searching for another prompt prey. The last similarity is the best case of how we ought to get a chance. Also, as far as pay opportunity, this model is proportional to an automated revenue opportunity.

Passive income open door can be perceived through cautious investigation of the financial condition that influences the hazard remunerate proportion of a specific speculation instrument. On the off chance that you are putting resources into financial exchange, the correct open door is the point at which the estimation of an organization that you are eager to purchase is at the base. For this situation, it is shabby and the potential for stock valuation is high. Along these lines, this is another passive income opportunity. In securities exchange, we procure from the profits of an organization and simultaneously from it's valuation. Exploiting the value change offers a great deal of passive income openings. In a perfect world, we purchase shares when they are modest and we sell them when they are costly. This is additionally valid with practically all exchanging instruments. An automated revenue opportunity is obvious when an unmistakable and solid pattern has been framing. To get the correct passage, we should comprehend why such variances happen with the goal that we can pursue where the market is going. It is essential to realize the value activity of an offered instrument to quantify the potential and the breaking point of an passive income opportunity and this is dictated by the changing elements of the market driven by a wide range of variables that we should likewise get into profoundly.

Brokers utilize two strategies to break down an passive income opportunity and these are called key and specialized investigation. Principal investigation is a technique for contemplating the current financial elements that influence the conduct of the market. At the point when the financial condition is great, it guarantees development for a specific venture. Along these lines, dealers are eager to purchase appealing instruments. What's more, thusly, they impact the remainder of the market players to drive the cost up.

In any case, when the financial condition is more awful, it drives fears and this is known as hazard avoidance. The previous is known as hazard hunger.

We can gauge the quality and shortcoming of the economy utilizing financial markers discharged intermittently. One of the most well known financial pointers is the GDP. At the point when the GDP number is higher than the gauge, the economy is solid and is reasonable for speculation. Another persuasive pointer is the joblessness rate. At the point when the joblessness rate is higher, purchasers are hesitant to spend. Organizations endure. Thus, it turns into an awful time for venture. This is only a model that every datum is significant for dealers so as to settle on steady choice. Great monetary markers present an automated revenue open door for financial specialists and brokers also.

Monetary updates on the sort can impact showcase suppositions. Be that as it may, some of the time, gossipy tidbits cause the merchants to respond more than the news does. In this way, most dealers purchase on bits of gossip and sell on news. This is likewise another zone for an passive income opportunity. How can it work? In the event that, for example, an organization was said to present an extremely focused item, speculators would purchase that organization a lot prior. Subsequently, the estimation of the organization would likewise get higher. What's more, if the news was not valid, early purchasers would sell and take their benefit. Thus, data gives us an automated revenue opportunity.

Another technique that dealers use to distinguish an passive income open door is the utilization of specialized investigation. Specialized examination gives brokers recorded information communicated in graph. Diagram can show distinguishing designs that help merchants pursue the course of the market. It additionally gives a sign if the cost of an exchanging instrument has arrived at a specific level where an inversion happens each time it is there. An automated revenue opportunity in specialized examination starts when the outline demonstrates a reasonable pattern directly after an inversion. Specialists in this field have various devices to uncover an automated revenue opportunity. Here, value moves inside an exchanging range. Be that as it may, when the range is broken, it suggests an a lot more grounded pattern. This is known as "break out". A break out circumstance is a major automated revenue opportunity. Purchasing on break out has demonstrated to be gainful.

Whatever strategy we use whether key or specialized, there is constantly an passive income opportunity.

There are as yet different approaches to locate an automated revenue opportunity, for example, the issues of new exchanging instruments. These incorporate IPO, government security selling and any crisp issue of speculation instrument. The main concern here is that since it is a crisp issue, the cost is at its least expensive and there is no heading than to go up.

First sale of stock (IPO) is a crisp issue of offers for an organization's development. Organizations don't need to obtain cash from banks to grow their activity. Rather, they will search for financial specialists to take care of up their assets to subsidize the development activity. This new issue has not yet been exchanged the securities exchange. At the point when an organization leads its IPO, the crisp issue of offers is purchased by speculation banks. Speculation banks will pay the organization a while later. At that point, the crisp issue which the speculation bank has purchased will be sold in the exchanging floor of the stock trade. This sort of offer in the exchanging floor is known as IPO. Why numerous brokers want to purchase an IPO is on the grounds that most organizations that issue IPO are in extension mode. Clearly, an organization extends when it has been developing, and the potential development in the close to term is high. Likewise, an IPO of a developing organization is offered at the base cost. Accordingly, the value bearing is set to a bullish pattern. After the first sale of stock, these offers will be exchanged. What's more, when these offers are moved starting with one dealer then onto the next, these offers will end up optional stocks. Initial public offering is one genuine case of passive income opportunity. In the securities exchange, gossipy tidbits about an IPO invigorate chance hunger. During financial log jam, IPO is not really heard except if the business it has a place with is flexible. In this way, an automated revenue opportunity starts when the economy has consistently been developing particularly if the primary beneficiary is the organization that issues the IPO.

Organization mergers and procurement likewise makes an automated revenue opportunity since it is constantly alluring to put resources into the monster.

As a set up advertiser, you're probably going to have things you can connect immediately to get progressively aloof money after some time. It's simply a question of putting the bits of the riddle together such that works.

The initial step is to check out what you have. What items do you have? What sites or area names do you have accessible? What are your aptitudes and what sort of Internet advertising knowledge have you developed? We at times become so smug with what we have that we overlook our potential. I realize I've done it commonly.

In some cases I'll glance through my rundown of items and state, "hello! I just advanced that on more than one occasion and it's extremely extraordinary." I at that point discover approaches to give new life to old items. I may put it all alone area, produce partner intrigue, reuse the substance in another spot, etc. It was a Jimmy D. Dark colored training item that instructed me to get all that you can out of what you compose - use it wherever you can to make as much from it as you can.

That is really what I need you to do as an initial step. Experience what you have and consider ways you can transform it into an automated revenue stream - or to increase what it's gaining you inactively at the present time.

One error I see numerous Internet advertisers making is just putting their items available to be purchased at the Warrior Forum. That just gets you up until now. Individuals truly won't see your item any longer sooner or later (except if it so happens to rank in the web crawlers for a key term, which works). Put that thing all alone space. Give it new life, another advancement, and another opportunity to inactively gain for you.

Now and again, you can take items you've made and use them as rundown developers. This is something I expect to do at this moment, really. Put my more established (yet still significant) items up as a complimentary gift in return for individuals' email address. This will at that point transform into an passive income worker where it wasn't previously.

Investigate the direct mail advertisements you have running too. It is safe to say that they are tantamount to they can be? Now and again, tidying your direct mail advertisement up can have emotional advantages (get in touch with me on the off chance that you need a tidy up - I have low rates on direct mail advertisement revises and I can more often than not help with changes).

Think about where you have your items available to be purchased. On the off chance that it's simply with a standard PayPal catch, you're missing out. Most items will improve subsidiary help behind them. Put them up through JVZoo or an installment entryway like that and you'll have a greatly improved shot of getting members to join to advance your item.

It's a given that systems administration is a colossal piece of the game. It's a lot simpler to get subsidiaries out there acquiring for you if individuals know you and the nature of your work. In case you're not getting enough partners, it's a great opportunity to chip away at your methodology. This is unquestionably something I have to do - I have brilliant partners however could utilize a lot more for a superior easy revenue.

Alongside selling more items comes fabricating a greater rundown. In case you're not building a rundown as you sell items, you're truly passing up a major opportunity. It causes me to recoil when I consider to what extent it took me to interface the two. I've even known about individuals completing enormous advancements for them as Warrior Product of the Day yet they didn't do any rundown working alongside it - that is a large number of pick ins, gone.

Do what I referenced above too - utilize more established items as complimentary gifts to get more individuals to pursue your rundown. Everything cooperates to enable you to gain more cash.

Blogging for Passive Income

I pursued a blogging challenge kept running by John and Matt Rhodes in 2008. I am happy I did! While I've never done what's needed with workathomeformoms.net blog to transform it into a gigantic worker all alone, it's been in charge of numerous magnificent recruits to my rundown. Individuals have come to know and confide in me through my blog.

Numerous advertisers have a blog as command post, and you ought to also. Individuals falter to make a promoting blog since they feel it's so soaked. In any case, that doesn't make a difference to me by any stretch of the imagination. Nobody else has my accurate arrangement of encounters to share or my novel understanding. I believe it's incredible to have a blog regardless of what number of others do on a comparative point. In the case of nothing else, it goes about as a kind of treatment for you to get your considerations and emotions on showcasing out there.

It can enable you to sell your items, construct your rundown, manufacture trust in you as a specialist, etc. It's not something you need to invest a huge amount of energy doing - simply consider it.

Dynamic List Building

Alongside letting a portion of my automated revenue streams fade away, I additionally profoundly lament not being progressively dynamic about my rundown building.

Offering to and building an association with those on your rundown is so fulfilling. It tends to be an incredible automated revenue worker in the event that you set up an autoresponder succession that works hands-off once individuals sign up to your rundown. My very own large portion list individuals have originated from offers of my items and through sites - however there is a lot more I could have done throughout the years. Notice my notice, and make rundown constructing a need for automated revenue.

Participation Sites

Participation destinations are another incredible passive income worker - relying upon what you look like at it. Regardless of those advertisers who attempt to sell you on these as being absolutely detached and simple, they aren't generally. They take a ton of delicate love and care to continue onward.

So, they are awesome in light of the fact that you don't generally need to go out to discover new purchasers. The purchasers are there as long as they buy in. For whatever length of time that you offer some benefit, they'll be fulfilled.

Consider placing a portion of your past items into a participation site. Consider a subject people will need to get notification from you month to month on. My present enrollment site is called Writing That Rocks - I give two month to month issues on subjects identified with composing. It's not something I've advanced especially outside of my own rundown, yet it's an incredible little enrollment individuals love, and it has transformed into passive income for me (on the off chance that you don't check the time spent composition the new issues!). For this situation, 'aloof' signifies I'm not finding new purchasers for new items constantly - participation reestablishes on autopilot. This is valid for most enrollment destinations. It is anything but a hands-off latent worker.

Upsells

I've rambled about things I wish I'd done diverse en route as an advertiser. A unique little something is that I avoided utilizing upsells for a really long time. I generally felt like I'd irritate individuals in the event that I had them. All things considered, some may be irritated yet I think a lot more are grateful - in any event with the manner in which I do them. I will in general offer upsells that are exceptionally valuable and on-point. They aren't excessively expensive and they aren't only there to get individuals' cash - they are there to be useful.

When somebody purchases a result of mine nowadays, there is commonly an upsell. It's not something individuals are influenced to purchase and it produces extra salary, uninvolved.

In the event that you haven't included upsells or set up a genuine deals pipe now, try it out. You may be astonished by how much your salary develops.

Cross Promotion

By that equivalent token, I've regularly been timid with regards to cross advancing my stuff. I ought not have been! There is no disgrace in telling individuals about my other, truly significant, items and administrations. Truth be told, individuals regularly express gratitude toward me for telling them those different things are accessible.

Investigate the things you sell - do you simply offer them to individuals as an irregular, or do you allow them to realize that you sell different things they may like? You can even observe this among famous writers on Amazon - the savvy ones let individuals realize that they have different books available to be purchased too. This can drastically expand your easy revenue.

You can even make a center point for your items so individuals can keep awake to date on them.

Passive income as an Affiliate

You're an accomplished advertiser, so you've likely fiddled with member showcasing now. In case you're similar to me, you got disappointed with Google changes and the majority of that and may have given things a chance to wane a bit. Get again into the game! For whatever length of time that you are doing things the correct way (the manner in which Google has enjoyed up and down) it's as yet conceivable. I'm as of now patching up all inactive subsidiary pay subsequent to rejecting a ton of what I had out of dissatisfaction.

There are a few things that have consistently worked and that I accept consistently will. The first is having exceptionally fantastic substance. Google needs to serve content that is actually what their searchers need to see. Thus, you simply need to give that to them.

Something else that has consistently worked is remaining over patterns - including "dispatch jacking" as it has turned out to be known. It's entirely simple to jump onto mid-super dispatches as an associate, making deals through your blog or other web properties. Try it out for automated revenue.

Momentous?

My objective here isn't to give you momentous data. The individuals who are more current or less experienced likely found new things. Be that as it may, I request that you not set this item aside regardless of whether you didn't 'get the hang of' anything new. The thought is - do you do these things? Do you have the present and future pay you need to have? If not, it's a great opportunity to institute these things. It's entertaining - as I was composing this I begun to discover the gaps in my very own business. I trust it's helped you discover the gaps in your business, as well. At times, even little changes can have an immense effect.

"Automated revenue" stands apart as the most contemplated trendy expression with respect to lucrative procedures nowadays, essentially due to the 'quick money/rich' bid is has. The present exchange subject is the legend versus truth of automated revenue.

As Wikipedia says, Passive salary is a pay gotten all the time, with little exertion required to look after it. Pop culture characterizes the idea as "cash earned by doing essentially nothing".

My meaning of passive incomeis much similar to this: cash earned by means of any underlying speculation without other extra input (time/cash/exertion).

Presently, we should jump into our legend versus truth segment of the exchange. The most average thought for this specific point is - that you simply don't have to do any movement to procure by means of along these lines. The truth - a large number of individuals have had a go at producing productive automated revenue streams, just to be astounded by the measure of work/money or time required. So on the off chance that you have chosen to go down this street, ensure you have comprehended the realities behind your passive income techniques.

One prominent procedure about making latent profit, Affiliate Marketing, appears to be a straightforward technique to make money to a great deal individuals. Here's exactly how it functions: Online advertisers or bloggers advance an outsider's item by including a URL to the item all alone destinations. At the point when a guest taps on the connection and purchases through the outsider, the site proprietor procures some commission. Member Marketing is viewed as aloof in light of the fact that, hypothetically, salary is created just by putting the web connect to your site. In actuality, you need to discover a methodology to pull in perusers to your site, click on the connection and buy something, which will take a great deal of your time and exertion when you are simply beginning. In fair conclusion, it is generally a long haul process. It is ideal to prescribe/advance items that you really have down to earth involvement with, in various words, be straightforward while composing the audits.

An alternate methodology is by making some sort of data items: E-books/CD/DVD - and pause while money from the offers of the items comes in. It is some of the time advertised by the web based showcasing masters being a straightforward, sure to fire strategy to create an automated revenue stream. Be that as it may, while these data items can in the long run develop into a phenomenal income stream, it's scarcely an aloof movement. It takes a lot of endeavors to make the item, and it must be of the best quality, something that individuals hoping to discover. There's the wrong spot for junk out there. You have to consistently be focused on devoting loads of time, vitality and cash into your undertaking at the beginning. Likewise, you should assemble an excellent stage/group of spectators to put your items.

Other well known procedures incorporate purchasing portion of stocks or obtaining a rental and so forth to make passive income streams. Significant thing for every one of these procedures is - nothing can make you rich medium-term without having won a type of lotteries. Passive income streams can without a doubt be life changers, yet you just should give a lot of exertion, time and some cash at first, and remain by your arrangement for long haul objectives.

Building detached acquiring streams is a fine method to invest additional energy or contribute your additional money to guarantee a staggeringly productive return. You ought to unquestionably never anticipate that it should immediately change your life. All things considered, it is reasonable to contribute your available time attempting to make a book or make up something else which will make automated revenue to address your issues. The huge fixings you need to begin are endeavors and time.

Numerous individuals likewise accept that automated revenue achievement just is accomplished by individuals who can stand to deal with it full-time. This isn't really right. While the facts confirm that the additional time you can contribute, the more outcomes you'll accomplish, there is without a doubt a spot for people who can make it an exceptionally powerful second salary stream.

CHAPTER TWO
BASIC THINGS ABOUT DROP SHIPPING AND HOW TO START EARNING

What is Drop Shipping?

Dropshipping is the place you offer items to a client that you don't physically have in your stock. The client pays you and afterward you pivot and buy the item from a distributer at a decreased benefit. The distributer at that point sends the thing to your client, for the most part utilizing your arrival address. You have a benefit on the effect between what the client pays you and what you pay the distributer. This can be a truly productive and rewarding business, in the event that you comprehend what to do...

Stage 1: Before You Do Anything Else

The initial phase in beginning any new business is to plunk down and work out a field-tested strategy. It doesn't need to be some protracted investigation of each part of your new business, however it should be in any event a rundown of visual cues to give a thought of what it is and where it's going. You have to incorporate what items or administrations you will give to your clients. You additionally need to discuss who your potential clients are and why they would need to buy from you. You likewise should consider how you are going to market to your potential clients to attract them to your site. Most significant of all you have to make sense of where you are getting the money related assets for the beginning up of your business. This isn't as large an arrangement in an dropshipping business as it would be in a business that holds stock and ships out its very own product. On the off chance that you set aside the effort to work out a strong strategy than you will have a superior shot of accomplishment with your new business than somebody who is going into this visually impaired.

Stage 2: Where Are You Selling?

The following stage in beginning an dropshipping business is choosing where you are going to sell your items. The two primary choices is by framing your own site or by selling them on a bartering site, for example, Ebay. Either alternative is an incredible method to profit. On the off chance that you are better at composing extraordinary item portrayals that get purchasers amped up for the item and would prefer not to burn through cash on a site page than eBay may be the best thing for you. After you have increased a little salary you should feel free to begin your own site. In any case, just by having a site does not mean you will get clients. You should investigate promoting your site through web crawlers to truly get that traffic streaming to your store. Both of these alternatives are incredible, it just relies upon what you believe is best for you.

Stage 3: Choosing a Drop Shipper

Perhaps the hardest thing about beginning an drop shipping business is finding a legitimate drop shipper. The web is loaded up with trick craftsmen who are professing to be drop shippers when they truly aren't. Spots like Doba and Mega Goods state they are dropshippers however as a general rule they are center men who have a rundown of real drop shippers that they use. They charge you more than what the genuine merchants charge them to outsource. With the end goal for you to get the most reduced cost on product, you have to sidestep the center men and go directly to the merchants. You can do this by going to sites that give arrangements of trustworthy wholesalers that you can use in your business. Thusly you can promise you are getting unquestionably the least costs. The most ideal approach to do this is to join a site that gives you access to an index of respectable drop shippers. These drop shippers can auction you stock at half or more.

Stage 4: Making the Money

The last advance in setting up an drop shipping business is profiting. On the off chance that you do what I have revealed to you as of now and you put some work into your business, you will profit. It is extremely unlikely you can't, except if you don't attempt. The most significant thing that you can realize when making cash is to make sure to cover your government expenses. This isn't free cash and the administration must have their cut, much the same as in an ordinary activity. So ensure you counsel a bookkeeper and have every one of your affairs together before surge off and start making those millions.

Drop shipping is a kind of retail satisfaction technique. Rather than a store stocking items, it buys the items from an outsider provider. The items are then sent straightforwardly to the purchaser.

For the store, this is a generally uninvolved procedure. The shipper doesn't need to request stock or satisfy the requests in any capacity. Rather, the outsider provider deals with the item itself.

Drop shipping is extraordinary for business visionaries since it doesn't request as much as the customary retail model. You don't need to open a physical store, pay overhead, and stock items. Rather, you open an online customer facing facade and purchase discount from providers who as of now have items and distribution center space.

The dealer is chiefly in charge of picking up clients and preparing orders in dropshipping , which means you'll viably be a broker. In spite of this, you'll harvest the a lot of the benefit by increasing the things you sell. It's a basic plan of action and one that can be fulfilling.

A huge number of business people rush to drop shipping on the grounds that it requires less issue and cash to begin. That is likely for what reason you're intrigued! What's more, the best updates on all? With drop shipping , you can manufacture a business that is supportable in the long haul directly from your workstation.

Obviously, there are numerous downsides and points of interest, and it's significant that we take a gander at them before you start your own drop shipping web based business. When you comprehend the upsides and downsides of dropshipping , figuring out how to outsource viably will be a breeze.

Advantages of Drop shipping

Drop shipping is anything but difficult to begin. You don't should be a business master to begin. Truth be told, you don't require any earlier business experience! In the event that you set aside some effort to become familiar with the rudiments, you can begin rapidly and gain proficiency with the rest as you come.

Drop shipping is so natural since it requires almost no from you. You needn't bother with a distribution center to store items or a group to enable you to out. You don't need to stress over legging or sending either. You don't need to invest a specific measure of energy consistently on your store. It's shockingly hands-off, particularly once you get moving.

The majority of this implies you can begin your business today. You don't have to go through months preparing everything. You can begin getting everything ready for action inside merely hours.

You will require some basic information and the correct apparatuses and assets, and that is the reason we made this guide. When you've completed it, you'll be furnished with the learning you have to kick off your very own dropshipping business.

Drop shipping is anything but difficult to develop. As you scale up, your plan of action doesn't need to change especially by any means. You'll need to place more work into deals and advertising as you develop, yet your everyday will remain pretty much the equivalent.

One of the advantages of drop shipping is that the expenses don't soar when you scale. Along these lines, it's anything but difficult to continue developing at a quite quick rate. You don't need to contract a gigantic group either. Except if you need to gather a little group sooner or later, you can do nearly everything without anyone else's input.

Drop shipping doesn't request a great deal of capital. Since beginning an dropshipping business requires nearly nothing, you can begin with negligible assets. You can construct a whole business directly from your workstation, and you don't have to make any abnormal state ventures. Indeed, even as your business develops, your costs will be genuinely low — particularly when contrasted with conventional operational expense.

Dropshipping is adaptable. This is perhaps the greatest advantage. You get the chance to work for yourself and set your very own principles. It's by a wide margin one of the most adaptable professions that anybody can seek after.

You can telecommute with minimal in excess of a workstation, and you can work at the occasions that are most helpful for you. This is perfect for business visionaries who need a business that works for them. You won't need to twist around in reverse to complete things. Rather, you set your very own tone.

Dropshipping is likewise adaptable in that it gives you a great deal of space to settle on choices that work for you. You can without much of a stretch rundown new items at whatever point you need, and you can change your techniques on the fly. In case you're taking some time off, you can computerize everything to flee. You get the thought — the potential outcomes are boundless.

Drop shipping is anything but difficult to oversee. Since it doesn't expect you to make numerous duties, you can oversee everything with little issue. Like I stated, you can do everything without anyone else's input on the off chance that you need to. When you've discovered providers and gotten everything set up, you're for the most part capable only for your online customer facing facade.

Weaknesses of Dropshipping

Dropshipping has thin edges. One of the disservices of dropshipping is that you ought to expect low edges at first. This isn't to imply that it can't be beneficial, yet you ought to know that the item edge in certain specialties may be little.

This issue is particularly tricky when you're dropshipping in a super-focused specialty. When you're battling for clients' consideration, you can't stand to make the sort of benefits you need to. In the event that you pick the correct specialty, you'll see bigger edges. In specialties with lower rivalries, you'll have better edges, yet for the most part it will just get so great. That is the reason dropshipping depends on a considerable measure of offers to be beneficial.

Dropshipping can make request preparing troublesome. Dropshipping appears to be clear: the client orders, you process, and your provider satisfies. Furthermore, generally, it is basic.

Be that as it may, in case you're sourcing items from various providers, you may keep running into certain issues. Every one of your providers may utilize an alternate transportation arrangement, which shows an issue for both you and your clients. Expenses can get high, and transportation various items can be risky.

Various providers will likewise have various structures set up for handling and charging. Since you need to deal with the connection with your providers, this can get precarious.

Dropshipping doesn't give you a ton of control. With regards to stocking items, request satisfaction, and delivery, things are out of your hands altogether. One of the impediments of dropshipping is that you don't have much power over specific parts of the dropshipping procedure. You need to depend on your providers to do everything right and work consistently. This absence of control can be off-putting to certain business people, however it more often than not isn't an issue.

This fair implies when something turns out badly, it very well may be dubious to oversee. When everything goes well, it's magnificent. Be that as it may, when provider issues occur, you simply need to sit tight for them to be settled. This can now and then reason client maintenance issues, yet with the correct harm control, you can moderate the issues and downplay client stir.

Dropshipping makes client care all the more testing. This is another issue that happens when requests turn out badly or providers come up short. Since you're only the customer facing facade, it very well may be hard to deal with requests. Like I referenced previously, you don't have a ton of control, and that can display troubles with regards to the client care side of things.

One of the most awful drawbacks of dropshipping is that you need to assume the accuse when your clients gripe. You could be doing everything right and still keep running into issues if your providers are having issues.

Is Dropshipping for You?

As referenced previously, there are the two advantages and disadvantages of dropshipping , which means it isn't for everybody. This is particularly the situation for individuals who are searching for an easy money scam. Dropshipping won't do that for you, and in case you're moving toward it that way, it's likely not the best decision for you.

All things considered, about anybody can assemble an dropshipping business.

In any case, you may have one of these feelings of dread:

"I don't have a clue in the event that I have sufficient opportunity to begin a business."

"I would prefer not to hazard getting terminated from my normal everyday employment."

"I would prefer not to buckle down on dropshipping that I fail to meet expectations at my 9-to-5."

Fortunately you can put to such an extent or as meager into dropshipping as you need to. Here are two basic approaches.

Dropshipping as a Side Hustle

What is dropshipping fundamental intrigue? Since it's adaptable and it doesn't request much, it's the perfect side activity. Numerous business visionaries do dropshipping as an afterthought while they have a primary activity that gives consistent pay. You don't need to forfeit your normal everyday employment to seek after your fantasies of turning into a business visionary.

The main stress here is that your manager will keep you from having a side hustle, yet in all honesty, numerous organizations approve of it. You'll need to ensure you're free – get some information about your organization's arrangement on side organizations and audit any non-contend understandings you've marked. You likewise unquestionably need to guarantee there's no irreconcilable circumstance. In any case, in the event that everything looks at, at that point you're ready.

You don't have to commit an excessive amount of time and vitality to dropshipping , which means you'll likely have the option to take it on effortlessly. Stressed that your side hustle will cause you to fail to meet expectations? You don't need to be! You can spend just a few hours on your business consistently and still succeed.

Be that as it may, it's critical to know your breaking points. On the off chance that you routinely stay at work past 40 hours at your normal everyday employment and battle to discover time for significant day by day duties, you probably won't almost certainly give an dropshipping business the consideration it needs. Dropshipping doesn't require a great deal, however you do need to place genuine work into it and cut out time in your day for it.

Much of the time, it just takes a tad of time the executives and planning. A lot of dropshipping retailers deal with their fundamental and side employments effectively. You don't have to rest 3 hours every night or skip suppers to make it work. You'll have to make sense of a calendar that works for you and stick to it religiously.

Dropshipping as a Full-Time Ecommerce Business

One of the advantages of dropshipping is the adaptability. You can make your business as large or as little as you need it to be. Numerous dropshippers do it as an afterthought, but at the same time it's a suitable vocation way. On the off chance that you need to be a full-time dropshipping retailer, you can be!

It's anything but difficult to scale up your business with dropshipping , which means you can develop your business before long while minimizing expenses. When you've arrived at clients and gotten enough deals, you can move from dropshipping low maintenance to full-time. The best part is that you can get this going at whatever pace you need to.

Clearly, this is going to take more work, however the result is well justified, despite all the trouble. When you make sense of how to outsource viably, you won't need to stress over insecure income. An entrenched dropshipping internet business works predictably, and it can even feel like you're creating automated revenue.

What's more, since it doesn't occupy a great deal of time, you could even agree with on a particular position hustle while as yet being a full-time dropshipping retailer! The sky's the cutoff.

Perhaps you're feigning exacerbation right now at the idea of turning into a full-time dropshipper, yet there are a huge number of examples of overcoming adversity from business visionaries who began right where you are today. It doesn't take a degree in business or millions in funding to bring home the bacon from it.

The Dropshipping Process

I quickly went over what dropshipping is, yet you probably won't know precisely how it functions. So here's a bit by bit diagram of the whole dropshipping procedure. I'll go over what it resembles in the background, and I'll additionally take a gander at what the client encounters (and why it makes a difference).

The majority of this seems like a confused riddle, yet once you figure out how to outsource, it's a smooth procedure for everybody included. You, the dropshipping trader, can do everything remotely and never at any point contact a solitary item!

Give me a chance to repeat that you needn't bother with any business experience to open an dropshipping customer facing facade. It unquestionably helps, however it's redundant. Many sprouting business people absolutely never pursue their fantasies since they accept they need a MBA or years of experience. This is absolutely not the situation. One of the advantages of dropshipping is that you can figure out how to outsource as you come.

Even better, there are various assets that make dropshiping   simpler than any time in recent memory. For instance, this valuable video gives some incredible exhortation on beginning. You can have totally zero business experience and still effectively make a benefit. You'll have to become familiar with the ropes en route, and it will challenge on occasion, yet I trust it's more than justified, despite all the trouble.

Like I referenced before, you needn't bother with a grcat deal of assets to begin dropshipping . Since you comprehend what dropshipping   is, read on to discover what you have to begin!

As we at first cautioned, dropshipping   is certifiably not an ideal, calm approach to fabricate a fruitful business. The model has some distinct points of interest yet accompanies various implicit complexities and issues you'll should most likely address.

We'll be analyzing these issues – and how to best address them – in future sections. Fortunately with some cautious arranging and thought, the majority of these issues can be settled and need not keep you from structure a flourishing, gainful dropshipping business.

CHAPTER THREE

Basic thing about affiliate marketing and how to start earning

For the people who have drawn in with web business, you should familiar with partner publicizing and how it capacities. In any case, for the people who are looking for opportunities to make extra pay on the web, anyway new to web business may not clear with what accomplice promoting is about, and how they can take in significant pay online with this strategy. We ought to explore it to help the people who are new to web business appreciate it's strategy and the potential worthwhile open entryways that they can get from partner exhibiting to make extra pay on the web.

Member showcasing is a salary sharing undertaking between a webpage owner/online sponsor (known as auxiliary) and an online shipper. Under this game plan, webpage owner makes money by propelling things controlled by an online merchant; they will put promotion on his website or driving web traffic from various sources to his webpage or direct to the vendor introduction page. If an arrangement or a movement required by shipper, for instance, top off a structure (lead age), the accomplice will procure a commission which may reliant on the degree of the sell cost or a fixed total.

Both partner and vendor are benefitted under this game plan. It is a triumph win strategy: branches can offer to benefit online without the need their own one of a kind things. Customer help and thing movement will be managed by shipper; however, merchant will save their publicizing costs while getting their things prologue to the market through partners' site and their advancing activities.

Branches can benefit through backup publicizing in three distinct ways:

1. Pay-per-click. Branches put seller's ads at their site, and if it is click by the site visitors which provoking the vendor's site, the accomplice will get pay, the whole may contrast from a penny to dollars dependent upon the things and the commission given by the shippers.

2. Pay-per-bargain. Branch will conceivably obtain commission if an arrangement is made through uncommon association set at backup site or their promoting endeavors. The commission will commonly be a certain degree of the sell cost or a fixed aggregate paying little regard to the sell cost.

3. Pay-per-lead. Each time a potential customer registers at the broker site through partner association, the backup will get a commission reliant on this action. The commission for pay per-lead will routinely be a fixed aggregate pre-directed by the shipper.

Part exhibiting opens the open entryway for website owners and the people who are charmed to benefit online an exceptional strategy to secure money without truly having to "do" anything. All it incorporates is putting advancements at their site or running commercial fights using their branch associate, kick back and believe that advantage will come in. The backend package which incorporates portion getting ready, thing or organization movement and customer supports will be dealt with by the dealer.

Subsidiary promoting is income sharing plan of action that advantage both website admin and the online dealer. It gives a most straightforward approach to individuals who need to telecommute and procure their living from web to profit on the web.

On the off chance that you've been pondering - what is subsidiary promoting - this chapter could well be what you have been searching for. We're going to see what associate promoting is and how individuals use it to profit online either for a full-time pay or only for some additional pocket cash.

Subsidiary showcasing, basically, is tied in with selling other individuals' items. For instance, you have a shipper who has an entire arrangement of items. The shipper's items may dress, electronic hardware, phones, data or even pet nourishment. In the event that you sell an item for the dealer, at that point you will acquire commission.

So how might you sell the items? The most straightforward approach to begin offshoot promoting is to compose articles on themes that are identified with the thing that you need to sell. You can add these articles to an article database. In the bio segment of the article, you would put a connection through to your vendor's item with an exceptional connection that will catch that you sent the traffic. In the event that the individual purchases the item, at that point you will almost certainly acquire the commission.

On the off chance that you have a site officially, at that point you can simply include a connection that focuses back to the site of the vendor and will record that you sent the guest, when they make a buy, you will proceed the commission.

What are the items? There are a wide range of items that you can sell. There are a huge number of shippers who are selling a large number of items. You should simply pick an item that you are keen on either by and by or on the grounds that you believe you would get a commission that interests you.

There are web destinations that take into account presenting associate so dealers and furthermore give the organization of following the deals and making the installments. For instance, Clickbank is a site that takes into account vendors and subsidiaries needing to sell advanced items. Advanced items are typically data based and have low overheads; this can bring about the commission rate being higher than a physical item.

Another sort of item that you can sell is a month to month membership item. For instance, USA Today and the Wall Street Journal both offer a commission that will repeat month to month which is an exceptionally appealing offering for the individuals who like to win benefits from less exertion.

So you can connect through to various items or a wide range of traders and sell items with a related subject. This makes it simpler to get the eyes of a specific group of spectators on the web. With a promoting, it is essential to find who your objective market is and guarantee that your site is made open to them by making it accessible in spots that they will visit. When you increase a readership of your site, you will at that point be in a more grounded position to offer items to your perusers.

Member showcasing can be characterized as advancement and ad of items by an outsider in return for commissions for each deal that have occur. It is by all accounts confounded so I will give you a model what subsidiary promoting implies.

For instance you are keen on enchantment. It is your most loved side interest. You will purchase a ton of enchantment gear and you even get it on the web. You know a great deal of data on enchantment and you feel that you ought to do a business that is identified with enchantment.

So one day, you intend to set up a business on enchantment. Yet, you face the issues of not having enough cash-flow to begin your very own disconnected business. Regardless of whether you would like to do your online business, you don't have the foggiest idea how to make a site. So does that imply that you are not ready to work together?

The appropriate response is a gigantic NO. What you can do is that you can locate an enchantment site that offers partner programs. You will understand that the site would need more traffic to their site and they are eager to pay commissions for anyone who is happy to enable them to bring a deal to a close. You won't need to make your own site as they will give you a member interface which you can send the traffic to.

So now all you should do is that you join their partner program. You will be center around figuring out how to advance their item, allude new clients, gather your bonuses and you will in a flash be good to go. You will almost certainly do every one of these organizations without having your own items and you won't need to burn through a great deal of time raising cash-flow to have a disconnected business.

Despite the fact that subsidiary promoting is by all accounts basic in idea, it isn't in every case simple by and by. As like any sort of business, you should place in the work, responsibility and time to develop your business. Be that as it may, in the event that you are eager to submit, the final products that you will get will be more than what you have contribution to the primary spot. I trust that this digital book will give you a chance to have a more clear picture on what subsidiary advertising is about.

You have presumably caught wind of profiting on the web with Affiliate Marketing and considering what it is about and how you can take advantage of the chance. All things considered, having been doing member promoting for very nearly 10 years, I will separate it here for your advantage. What pursues is a finished manual for partner advertising and how you can profit from it.

Associate Marketing is the same old thing. It is just alluding individuals to purchase an item or administration as an end-result of a commission from the item merchant or specialist co-op.

Monetary administrations organizations like insurance agencies, banks, and resource chiefs have been utilizing it for a considerable length of time to manufacture their organizations. They may call their member advertisers autonomous advertisers and call the commission, execution rewards, however take it from me it is offshoot promoting.

Member Marketing may have existed for a considerable length of time, it didn't end up prevalent until the web occurred. With the web and expansion of web innovations, offshoot promoting ended up less difficult, pulling in more enthusiasm from individuals.

Partner advertisers never again needed to go thumping way to entryway to make a deal. They can basically release the intensity of web advances to advance the items or administrations of their customers.

At this point you realize I am concentrating on online subsidiary showcasing, in light of the fact that in spite of the fact that offshoot advertising should at present be possible disconnected, best associate advertisers influence web innovations.

To do partner promoting, you need a trader or an organization that offers associate showcasing opportunity or a subsidiary advertising program. Simply visit the site of the business and search for a connection that says Affiliates, Associates or Make Money.

You can likewise information exchange with an Affiliate Network like Commission Junction (presently CJ Affiliate by Conversant) or

ShareASale. These are administrations that offer a one-stop shop to various offshoot advertising programs. An Affiliate Network can have several projects to join, making it simple to discover subsidiary promoting openings.

The associate system offer following programming that tracks your deals and reports your deals and execution. They likewise handle your installment. More or less, a member system resembles an agent among dealers and partner advertisers.

However, How Does everything Work

When you information exchange to an associate program (regardless of whether legitimately from the shipper or through a subsidiary system), you are given special material which incorporates a connection and/or pennant and connections.

Your activity as a member advertiser is to advance these connections and pennants utilizing your blog, web based life pages, or internet publicizing. These associate connections lead to the shipper site and accompanies a following code that screens whether the lead purchases an item from the vendor.

At the point when an individual taps on your advanced connection, a sign is sent to your offshoot program's server advising them of the alluded visit and a little bit of code called a treat is put away on the PC or cell phone of the client.

This treat accompanies a fall to pieces clock. The treat will stay dynamic on your customer's gadget until the check down hits zero after-which the treat is erased. To what extent a treat remains dynamic is out of your hands, it is dictated by the subsidiary program.

Treat break for a subsidiary program can be as low as 24 hours for projects like Amazon or as long as 30 days for projects like Jumia and Gearbest. A few projects can have their treat dynamic for as long as 90 days.

You may now think about what the lifetime of a treat has to do with anything.

Here is the thing

A subsidiary deal must be credited to you if the treat is as yet dynamic on your lead's gadget when they purchase the item.

Presently, an Example

Suppose you are an individual from Gearbest partner program and you imparted their connection to your companions on Facebook and one of them taps on your connection, a treat with a 30-day break is put away on their gadget.

In the event that the lead purchases 20 days after the underlying snap, the treat will at present be dynamic (10 days to go). The deal will be related to you and you will win a commission on whatever item they purchased whether it was a similar item you advanced.

Presently, Another Example

Suppose the situation is equivalent to above, yet for this situation, the lead holds up 35 days before purchasing (for example 5 days after your treat planned out). Your treat is gone, the deal can't be related to you. No commission for you for this situation.

Thus, similar to I referenced later in this article, treat break is something to think about when picking an offshoot program. Pick a partner program that gives you a sensible time to make a deal.

When you make the payout furthest reaches of the partner program or subsidiary system, you will be equipped for installment inline with the installment cycle of the program.

Sorts of Affiliate Marketers

I know, you might ponder whether there are more than one kind of offshoot advertiser. However, for most settled advertisers, there isn't generally any qualification.

Be that as it may, to serve tenderfoots getting to associate showcasing open doors just because, I think that it's convincing to make this little qualification. This will empower you know where you are at the present time and what approach will enable you to get to progress quickest.

Here are two sorts of Affiliate Marketers:

Item Centric Affiliate Marketers

Content Centric Affiliate Marketers

How about we make a plunge somewhat more profound

1. Item Centric Affiliate Marketers

Customarily, this is the thing that partner showcasing is about. You discover an item you like and you utilize distinctive showcasing channels to advance it. You can manufacture a site around the item or specialty the item has a place with.

You could manufacture web based life pages or gatherings around this item, Create a YouTube channel, purchase advertisements on Facebook and Google, make email promoting, and deals pipe all to drive deal to this item and acquire attractive commissions. You could be doing this for numerous items and administrations at the same time.

As an item driven subsidiary advertiser, you are tied in with selling the item or administration. You get up every morning looking into items to sell or techniques to sell a greater amount of your present items.

You could assemble many little specialty sites each focused at an item you sell. You may not have a site by any means. You can simply purchase advertisements from Social Networks, Search

Engines, and other traffic sources to direct people to your offshoot items and administrations.

In any case, ensure that the expense of offer does not surpass deals. You would not have any desire to make $100 in the wake of burning through $150 in Ads and different deals costs.

Content Centric Affiliate Marketers

Content Centric Affiliate Marketers are individuals who have fabricated a crowd of people by making standard substance on the web and now use associate showcasing as one of the methods for adapting their substance creation.

You may have a blog about pets or a YouTube channel where you talk magnificence. You may even simply be sharing your photographs on Instagram or Facebook and have amassed heaps of fans.

Your energy is to share your substance and construct your image, partner advertising is only one way you profit from that enthusiasm.

When you get up in the first part of the day, you are considering what new (content, photographs, recordings) to wow your crowd and manufacture your notoriety on the web. Obviously, as you go further into partner advertising what item that will offer best to your group of spectators will have some effect on your substance creation.

While, I see item driven offshoot advertisers as expert partner advertisers, I will in general observe content-driven associate advertisers as unintentional subsidiary advertisers.

There is nothing amiss with this, in certainty I consider myself to be even more a substance driven subsidiary advertiser. As you go on in your voyage in partner showcasing you will eventually fuse the two ways to deal with your methodology.

Today I utilize the two techniques, however I tend towards substance than item.

Presently, here are a couple of interesting points when picking an Affiliate Marketing Program:

1. Would i be able to Sell the Product/Service

When picking a partner showcasing system pick one that sell the sort of items and administrations that you can advance effectively on the web. To sell an item you must persuade. In the event that you are not well tremendous about an item, you will think that its troublesome persuading others to purchase.

In the event that you have a site or a stage (like Instagram, Facebook, YouTube, and so on) with a current group of spectators, you ought to pick member showcasing programs with items or administrations that will speak to your crowd.

Try not to pick an associate showcasing program basically in light of the fact that it pays more commissions as you might be paid on the off chance that you can effectively sell the item.

2. Does the Program bolster my Country

While most subsidiary advertising projects bolster nations like USA, Canada UK, and European nations, some member projects may not bolster nations like Nigeria or some African and Asian nations. Henceforth, when picking a partner program pick one that supports your nation.

You might be enticed to guarantee you are from another nation, yet you need to recollect that if an offshoot does not bolster your nation, your profit won't be sent to you in your nation. Attempting to compromise, may make it troublesome or difficult to get your profit.

3. What are the installment choices?

Identified with help for nation is installment alternatives. In the event that the installment alternatives upheld by your offshoot promoting project are not bolstered in your nation, you won't most likely get your installments. Thus, before selling for a member, ensure you will probably get your cash.

Most prominent installment choices offered by partner projects incorporate Checks, Wire Transfer, PayPal, Payoneer, and Direct Deposit,

The surest method to get your associate profit in Nigeria is through wire move or direct store. Payoneer is additionally a choice.

While PayPal is one of the most helpful installment stages, they don't support getting installments in certain nations (for example Nigeria). Thus, ensure getting installment is authoritatively bolstered by PayPal in your nation before joining an Affiliate program that has PayPal as the main installment channel.

4. Does it Offer Sale Support?

Your subsidiary program should enable you to succeed, after the entirety of your prosperity is their prosperity. They should give you state-of-the-art data about your navigate and deals, so you can without much of a stretch comprehend what is working and what isn't.

Your associate advertising project ought to likewise furnish you with data and instructional exercises on the best way to prevail in your business. Pick an associate that has a blog, client gatherings and discussions that will enable you to succeed.

A decent offshoot program ought to likewise furnish you with deals materials like pennants and content connections (Marketing and Promotion support), so you can concentrate on your primary occupation Promotion.

The site of the dealer ought to likewise be all around planned with the goal that your leads will have a decent encounter when they get to the site. This will enable you to sell more.

5. How dependable is the Affiliate Program (Reputation)

When picking a partner program to join, start with traders with a decent notoriety. This makes your activity simpler as you should simply point leads at them. Their great notoriety will make individuals to believe them enough to purchase, which will bring about more deals for you.

Pick a member promoting program with a dependable framework. The framework for following requests and deal must be dependable. Do they pay immediately? What is their nature of administration? Quest on the web for news and audits about the shipper you need to join its program and check whether they have positive or negative exposure.

Quest for your preferred subsidiary program on Google with a trick capability. Model, you could look through GoDaddy Affiliate Scam.

6. At the point when will you get paid

You ought to consistently affirm the installment system of an offshoot program before joining. You ought to pose inquiries like

What is the base parity you should gather before you are paid (Minimum Payout sum or Payment Threshold)?

How regularly would you be able to get Payment (Weekly, Monthly, like clockwork)?

What is the Payment Cycle? for example At the point when does representing deals gets secured and to what extent from that point will you get installment for secured deal.

7. What is the Cookie Timeout

Like I clarified before, the treat break decides to what extent from the time you originally indicated a lead a subsidiary dealer's site that a buy from them will win you a commission.

Treat Timeout can be 24 hours, multi week, two weeks, 30 days, or as long as 90 days or significantly more.

7. What is the Commission Structure

You likewise need to discover what level of commission you get for making a deal. Is it a level commission on all deal or commission relies upon the classification of the item.

Something else to be vigilant for is whether the commission is a one-time commission, repeating commission, or remaining commission.

Once commission implies that you can possibly gain once for a buy regardless of whether the lead purchases again in future utilizing your member connection or they continue paying for the progressing utilization of the item or administration just like the case with memberships.

Repeating commission implies you can win the same number of times you carry a lead to the shipper.

Lingering commission happens for the most part with some membership based subsidiary projects. You continue procuring commission as long as the lead you acquired continues paying their membership. At some point this may go on inconclusively or inside a specific time allotment, state a half year or 1 year.

8. What Promotion Channels are Permitted

It is additionally a smart thought to discover various ways the subsidiary program permits you advance their items. Some may deny promoting on Search Engines like Google others may glare against utilizing web based life.

In a couple of cases they may not boycott Advertising on web indexes completely, they may simply forbid you seeking certain catchphrases in your inquiry promoting effort.

You have to ensure that your techniques for advancement are allowed by the member program.

You can advance items and administrations on a current site or blog or you can discover an item and fabricate a site around it. On the off chance that you as of now have a site with a sizable group of spectators, you can begin by collaborating with offshoot programs that are significant in your specialty. This could enable you to test and tear accomplishment from associate showcasing quicker.

In the event that you don't have a site, you simply need to construct one particularly on the off chance that you mean being in member promoting for the long run. You don't really require a site, yet having one gives more control and a bit of leeway.

A site is the main moral approach to construct your email list, which is the contribution of your business channel that will acquire profoundly important leads. You may not begin with a site, yet have it in your arrangement to have at any rate one site.

Most offshoot advertisers have various sites with each focused to a specialty and used to sell items and administrations applicable to the specialty.

A specialty site works best with offshoot promoting. It is engaged to a specialty, consequently just individuals keen on the specialty will visit the site, which means they will all the more decidedly react to advancements on the off chance that they are important to the specialty.

Nonetheless, don't wrongly think a specialty must be little. Innovation is a specialty so is memory card. Design is a specialty, so is high-eel.

Building a Website

WordPress is the best stage for structure sites and web journals. It is anything but difficult to introduce and has heaps of modules that will empower you construct any kind of site you need.

To assemble a site, you need facilitating administrations. This can cost somewhere in the range of $10 every month to $30 every month. Checkout my suggestions for best web facilitating.

You additionally need an area name, which can cost you about $10 every year. You can see my rundown of best benefits for Domain name Registration.

You can arrangement the site yourself or in the event that you would prefer not to be exhausted with the specialized subtleties, you can pay a website specialist or consultant to assist you with the arrangement.

For data of the cost ramifications of owning a site, read this far reaching article about the expense of structure a site.

When your site is prepared, post significant substance on your site with the goal that you keep your perusers drew in and pull in progressively important guests. You can do the keeping in touch with yourself or you can draw in an independent essayist to make the substance.

You ought to likewise focus on the most recent advancement in site improvement (SEO) to enable you to pull in more search traffic. Remember to coordinate your site with Google Analytic to get helpful data about your crowd.

Likewise register with Webmaster apparatuses from Google, Bing, and Yandex to get some helpful data about the SEO soundness of your site. You ought to likewise checkout my nitty gritty article on the best way to begin a blog.

Step by step instructions to Build Traffic to Blog or Website

Directed traffic is extremely significant to prevailing in member showcasing. The more focused on traffic you can drive to your site, the more the business you can make. Here are two or three different ways to manufacture traffic to your partner showcasing site.

1. Site improvement

Site design improvement empowers your site rank better on Search Engines like Google for important watchwords in your specialty. It is tied in with putting all the correct flag in your substance and your site to make Google see it and rank it better for pertinent watchwords.

With a decent arrangement for your site on Google SERP pages, you will draw in more visits, which is useful for subsidiary promoting, particularly on the off chance that it is focused on. Search engine optimization is a significant achievement factor in partner showcasing and everything begins with the substance.

Here are a couple of tips for composing SEO-agreeable substance:

Know Your Keywords: Every post must objective at least one watchwords. Before composing a substance you need a catchphrase as a main priority. This is the place Keyword Research comes in. Utilizing apparatuses like Ahrefs, you can discover watchwords important to your offshoot advertising specialty.

Target One Keyword at once: Each article or bit of substance should target one fundamental catchphrase. You can add a couple of auxiliary watchwords to enable you to catch groups of long tail catchphrases identified with your fundamental catchphrase. Try not to be capricious with your substance creation. Each bit of substance ought to have an unmistakable reason with a catchphrase as its special personality.

Utilize the Keyword in Important pieces of the substance: In the tip above I prescribed that you target one primary catchphrase. You may now ask how. By utilizing it in your substance and including it in all the correct spots. Your watchword ought to show up in the title, in the primary passage, in the last section, and in the middle. Don't anyway stuff your substance with catchphrases as web indexes are currently keen enough to distinguish such contrivance. Likewise incorporate into the alt-content of pictures.

Use Hierarchy in your Content: Use headers and subheaders to indicate connections between the various areas of your substance. This makes your substance simpler for your guests to peruse, which is sure for your member promoting achievement.

The more joyful they are with your substance the more probable they are to stay to view and ideally click on your member advancements. Headers are additionally extraordinary for web search tools as it gives valuable signs that helps internet searcher better comprehend what your substance is about. Remember to include your primary catchphrase and auxiliary watchwords in a portion of the headers.

Fabricate Internal Links: When composing another substance, discover more established substance that are pertinent to your present substance and include connections pointing at them. Don't simply advance your subsidiary showcasing joins, likewise advance your more established substance. When the article is done, you can likewise connection to it from a portion of your more seasoned substance. Ensure you utilize the fundamental catchphrase in the stay content of the inside connection

Utilizing the tips above will go far to enable you to make content that are web crawler prepared. Be that as it may, it probably won't be sufficient.

Third party referencing

Every one of the tips given above are all piece of what is approached site SEO. Be that as it may, nearby SEO isn't generally enough for a novice. This is the place off-site SEO comes in. The best off-site SEO is third party referencing.

Third party referencing is significant in light of the fact that, the number, quality, and pertinence of connections indicating any substance is a significant positioning variable utilized by Google. When your substance is nearby SEO agreeable, a little third party referencing will help its situation in the inquiry positioning, which is all you have to prevail in associate promoting.

Systems for third party referencing include:

Visitor Posting

Posting on Relevant Communities (Forums, and so forth)

Blog Commenting

2. Evergreen Content

Compose content that individuals search constantly. This guarantees once you rank well in web crawlers you will get consistent traffic from the substance. Also, in light of the fact that old substance continues turning in guests, your traffic will undoubtedly develop as you include increasingly applicable substance.

Interestingly, newsy substance expects you to push out heaps of substance, since news more often than not have short life cycles, the vast majority are not inspired by them following a few days. This implies you need to continue producing content ordinarily to get traffic.

With evergreen substance you can compose more than once per month can at present get heaps of traffic in the event that you handle your on location and off-site SEO bit well.

Best Content Types for Affiliate Marketing with your Website

A wide range of substance won't go well with subsidiary showcasing. For instance news site and tattle web journals will battle to prevail with member promoting.

This is on the grounds that the substance isn't focused on and most guests are essentially there for the essence and to lash out on one another in the remark area. Evergreen substance is the best methodology for structure content for associate showcasing on your site.

Presently, here are the best sorts of evergreen substance for Affiliate Marketing

1. How Tos

With "How tos" you distinguish an issue in your specialty and give an itemized arrangement on the most proficient method to fathom it. To take care of the issue, certain items and administrations might be required.

Your activity as a member advertiser is to distinguish the best items offered by your offshoot showcasing accomplices for taking care of this issue and suggest them inside the article.

2. Tips

Tips are like How Tos and work similarly. You give two or three hints and after that prescribe several items or administrations important for the tip to be effectively executed.

3. Correlation

You can likewise compose an article looking at least two related items or administrations. In the article you feature the advantages and disadvantages of every item. Obviously, you include connections of the items or administrations from your associate showcasing accomplices.

4. Audits

In an audit, you expound on a decent quality item you as of late utilized. You share the highlights of the item or administration with your clients.

You additionally feature what you like and detest about the item or administration and incorporate connects to your associate promoting accomplices where intrigued guests can purchase the item or administrations.

Member Marketing Success Difficult with News and Gossip/Viral Websites

In view of an absence of focused traffic it is hard to prevail in partner promoting if the sum total of what you have is a news or viral site. News sites more often than not have a differing traffic making it hard to focus on your group of spectators.

Another issue with news locales is the expectation of their guests. At the point when individuals visit news locales they will probably peruse the news not to purchase an item. Along these lines, offshoot advertising advancement on a news site intrudes on the common progression of the guests.

News destinations get more straightforward traffic as guests as a rule get through the landing page. Notwithstanding when they come through inquiry, they are utilizing terms identified with the brand of the viral site as opposed to looking for a particular item, administration, or arrangement.

This is the reason evergreen substance works best. They are focused at taking care of a specific issue. Subsequently the client as of now has an aim to take care of the issue. Along these lines, if the item or administration behind your subsidiary showcasing advancement will take care of this issue for her, she will be increasingly responsive.

Internet based life is another successful method for advancing your offshoot items and administrations. You most likely as of now have some group of spectators via web-based networking media, you can begin from that point. Like with structure sites, having a Facebook page or gathering that is engaged to a specialty is probably going to be increasingly powerful.

Notwithstanding, on the off chance that you are an influencer or a big name, you basically need to advance items and administrations you really like. As an influencer or VIP your fans will react to your suggestions essentially in light of the fact that they like or trust you. Simply ensure you really like the item and it is of good quality or you will face reaction from your fans.

It is likewise significant that each post isn't an advancement. Try not to yield in distributing those fascinating and connecting with substance that helped you assemble that crowd in any case or you may lose them.

Offshoot Marketing on Facebook

Facebook is the most well known person to person communication stage. It is probably the best stage to do offshoot advertising. Simply share important items and administrations of your subsidiary organizations with your companions and fans and various them could wind up purchasing.

Be that as it may, Facebook has been securing natural commitment in the course of the most recent few years in their offer to lift promoting deals. This implies to get some footing with Facebook, you will most likely require some promoting spending plan. Simply ensure that the expense of offer does not surpass deals.

Various offshoot advertisers are presently going to Facebook Groups to advance their partner connects as natural commitment is as yet positive in Facebook Groups. Be that as it may, to what extent Facebook's sentiment with Groups will last is unsure, making depending on Groups not a practical system.

You don't need a ton of fans to showcase on Facebook. All you need is a Facebook page and you can approach the informal organization's 2.2 billion dynamic month to month clients.

You can do various things with your Facebook Ad. You can go-to people straightforwardly to the presentation page of your offshoot program. You could likewise guide them toward your site where you presumably have an information exchange structure for structure the email show you requirement for your email promoting effort.

While Facebook has over 2.2 billion dynamic clients, not every person of them will react decidedly with your partner showcasing and attempt to sell something. You have to utilize the instruments given by Facebook to focus on your Ads just to buyers who bound to purchase whatever it is you are selling.

Offshoot Marketing on Instagram

The issue with sharing your offshoot items and administrations on Instagram is that the photograph amicable internet based life stage does not permit you add connects to your posts. Indeed, the main connection permitted on Instagram is the one on your profile.

A powerful technique that many offshoot advertisers use to advance their associate organizations on Instagram is to put the member connect in their profile for the span you will run the battle. That way, your guests can tap on the connection on the profile.

Since the connection is included crude, it is smart thought to utilize a URL shortening administration like goo.gl to make the connection increasingly adequate.

Member Marketing on YouTube

YouTube is the most prominent internet searcher for recordings. YouTube is additionally the biggest web based life stage for Videos. This double nature makes YouTube a compelling wellspring of traffic for offshoot showcasing.

The technique utilized by partner advertisers is to make a video control, tip, how to, or survey of the item or administration you need to sell. At that point in the portrayal you add connects to the item utilizing your partner interface.

Remember to illuminate your watchers that you have incorporated a connect to the item or administration for their benefit. This will prompt a higher active visitor clicking percentage.

Member Marketing with Email Marketing

Email showcasing is another successful method to advance your associate organizations. It is one that most masters use. The principal phase of email promoting is building an email list. This is a rundown of email locations of leads and clients.

In case you are a present business and starting at now have email areas of your customers on record, you can start with this once-over. The best technique to create an email summary is through a select in structure on your site. The pick in structure is the segment reason for your business pipe.

The basis behind the select in structure is essential: offer your visitors something of critical worth in vain and demand that they enter their email address in the structure with the objective that you can send them the free offer.

If what you are offering is of worth most customers will enter their email. The email you assemble thusly ends up being a bit of your email list that you can use to send uncommon substance.

For email elevating to be practical in your auxiliary exhibiting exertion, you need to section your gathering of observers. This will enable you center around the reasonable courses of action and offers to the right gathering of observers which will realize more arrangements.

You can checkout a few email displaying providers like Aweber, that will empower you to mechanize your illuminating. They can moreover help with following, personalization, and division.

Tips for Affiliate Marketing Success

Here are two or three hints to extend the difference in your part advancing endeavors:

Be Contextual

One way to deal with win at partner displaying is to ensure that the headways you are sharing is relevant to the substance and your gathering of observers. Propelling shoes on a page about how to buy a shoe will have more change than on a page about how to buy a phone.

Guarantee the partner notices you are propelling match the substance.

Accordingly, share your headways on critical internet systems administration pages, get-togethers, YouTube channels, etc

Be Authentic

Recommend simply incredible quality things and organizations. Don't over offer a thing or untruth to get people to buy. Essentially present the substances in a persuading way.

Misleading your gathering of onlookers will incite a breakdown in trust which is amazingly terrible for your part promoting accomplishment. Being true blue will grow trust and help you develop your reputation.

Use Deep interfaces

Part displaying projects commonly offer associations and banners to make it straightforward for you to start propelling their things and organizations. The issue with these constrained time materials is they are by and large showing the point of arrival or a grouping page, which is ordinarily too much traditional.

For best results use significant association gadget (offered by most extraordinary accomplice programs) to point to the unmistakable thing or organization you have to progress. This is in like manner in the spirit of the chief tip (Be Contextual). The significant association gadget will enable you convert any thing interface from the dealer site to a partner association.

Traffic is Important, yet Targeted Traffic is King

Try not to concentrate a lot on crude traffic. With Affiliate showcasing the purpose of the group of spectators for connecting with the substance matters. This is the reason a 100 visits from a focused on traffic source like pursuit will as a rule outflank 1000 visits from a viral traffic source.

Ensure your substance is seen more by individuals who have a purchasing aim and you will be effective with partner showcasing.

Track your Performance

Try not to do your offshoot advertising blind. Discover the kinds of items individuals are reacting to and offer business as usual. Most great associate systems will offer input on items being sold or possibly the class.

Now and then, guests might search for items on your site that you as of now don't cover. Thinking about these substance holes opens new winning open doors for you.

Use instruments like Google Analytics and Google Search Console to track substance holes and when you discover them, construct extraordinary substance to fulfill your guests.

CHAPTER FOUR
HOW TO INVEST AS SOMEONE INTERESTED IN PASSIVE INCOME

Easy revenue, more or less, is cash that streams in all the time without requiring a considerable measure of exertion to make it. The thought is that you make a forthright speculation time as well as cash, however once the ball is moving, there's insignificant support required going ahead. That being stated, not all passive income open doors are made similarly. For speculators, fabricating a strong portfolio means knowing which inactive contributing methodologies to seek after.

1. Land

Regardless of some high points and low points as of late, land keeps on being a favored decision for financial specialists who need to create long haul returns. Putting resources into an investment property, for instance, is one approach to create a customary wellspring of pay. At the beginning, a speculator might be required to set up a 20% up front installment to purchase the property, yet that may not be a hindrance for somebody who's as of now sparing normally. When solid inhabitants are introduced, there's next to one side to do aside from sit tight for the lease checks to start coming in.

Land speculation trusts (REITs) are another aloof venture choice for financial specialists who aren't keen on managing the everyday weight of dealing with a property. One of the primary focal points of a REIT is that they pay out 90% of their assessable pay as profits to financial specialists. There is a drawback, be that as it may, since profits are saddled as normal salary. That might be tricky for a financial specialist who's in higher a duty section.

Land crowdfunding presents a center ground arrangement. Financial specialists have their decision of value or obligation interests in both business and private properties. In contrast to a REIT, the financial specialist gets the expense favorable circumstances of direct proprietorship, including the devaluation reasoning with no of the additional obligations that accompany owning a property.

2. Shared Lending

The shared loaning (P2P) industry is a little more than 10 years old, and the market has developed significantly. For financial specialists who need to help other people while adding passive income to their portfolio, shared loaning is an appealing decision.

For a certain something, there are less hindrances to passage contrasted with different kinds of ventures. For instance, both Prosper and Lending Club, two of the biggest P2P stages, enable financial specialists to store advances with as meager as a $25 venture. The two banks likewise open their ways to non-licensed speculators. While Title III of the Jumpstart Our Business Startups (JOBS) Act permits both licensed and non-certify speculators to contribute through crowdfunding, each crowdfunding stage has its approach with respect to who can take an interest.

As far as the profits, shared loaning can be productive, especially for financial specialists who are happy to go for broke. Advances pay a specific measure important to financial specialists, with the most elevated rates related with borrowers who are considered the greatest credit chance. Returns regularly go from 5% to 12%, and there's next to no the speculator needs to do past financing the credit.

3. Profit Stocks

Profit stocks are probably the most effortless ways for speculators to make an passive income since you're successfully getting paid to claim them. As the organization gets income, some portion of them is redirected and paid back to speculators as a profit. This cash can be reinvested to buy extra shares or got as a money installment.

Profit yields can change enormously starting with one organization then onto the next, and they can likewise vary from year to year. Financial specialists who are uncertain about which profit paying stocks to pick should adhere to ones that fit the profit noble name, which means the organization has offered progressively higher profits sequentially over the past 25 years.

4. File Funds

File assets are common finances that are attached to a specific market record. These assets are intended to reflect the exhibition of the basic file they track, and they offer a few favorable circumstances over different ventures for financial specialists whose objective is automated revenue.

Record assets are inactively overseen, and the protections incorporated into them don't change except if the structure of the file changes. For financial specialists, this means lower the executives costs. Beside that, a lower turnover rate makes file subsidizes more assessment effective, decreasing drag that would somehow or another reduce returns.

The Bottom Line

Automated revenue speculations can make a financial specialist's life simpler from numerous points of view, especially when a hands-off methodology is liked. The four alternatives illustrated here speak to contrasting degrees of expansion and hazard. Similarly as with any speculation, it's critical to gauge the foreseen returns related with an automated revenue opportunity against the potential for misfortune.

On the off chance that you need to figure out how to make an automated revenue, it is first critical to know the meaning of easy revenue. Easy revenue, in less complex words, is winning cash from sources without your immediate inclusion. All things considered, you be included somewhat to start with, however then when the salary creating angles are set up, you will at that point have the option to go on to different activities, while that unique source keeps on acquiring cash for you.

There are numerous approaches to make an automated revenue both on the web, and off the web. One of the most prevalent ways is to get investment property. Contingent upon the age of the property, and the nature of the leaseholders, there will be some work required similar to upkeep and ordinary support. Not every person has the cash to put resources into property, or the abilities to do basically everything included. Be that as it may, the automated revenue from rental units can be worthwhile. Other basic wellsprings of this kind of salary are sovereignties that you will get for an innovation or inventive work. Genuine instances of individuals who are equipped for gaining along these lines are artists, on-screen characters, and App manufacturers. These are abilities which just a set number of individuals have, and having the option to bring home the bacon from this sort of automated revenue can be intense.

This is the place the excellence of the web turns into the closest companion of the shrewd, aspiring "customary" individual. For by far most of individuals who don't have the propelled gifts to be effective in expressions of the human experience, music, or film, however who are dedicated and persistent, there are numerous approaches to win inactively through the web. Normally, individuals join partner programs wherein they set up a site to sell a specific item. For every deal, the merchants get commissions. The dealer gives every one of the designs to the site, and they do practically everything of dealing with their item. You are just paid to have their connection on your site. In this inconvenient time of the worldwide economy, where promoting dollars are winding up increasingly rare, organizations are finding that publicizing on sites is huge business. For the site proprietor, it responds to the subject of how to make an automated revenue in the web.

Individuals who claim a site or blog with substantial traffic can put ads on their site. Step by step instructions to make an automated revenue along these lines originates from numerous sources. You may likewise participate in compensation per snap crusades which create a specific measure of salary with each snap. At the point when the site and blog substance is watchword rich, fascinating, and elegantly composed, odds are that it will turn out to be increasingly more prominent as time passes by. When great substance is out on the web, regardless of whether composed or put into a video, it is essentially ensured to remain out there for a considerable length of time, or more. The absolute best Online Entrepreneurs state that sites, articles, or YouTubes they have made even a long time before are as yet acquiring them huge easy revenue. As a rule, the salary really expands the more extended the substance is on the web.

In the past producing an automated revenue was confined to those with a great deal of beginning capital. The familiar axiom "You need cash to profit" is never again substantial. I need to tell you the best way to make an automated revenue stream without any preparation.

Property is extraordinary for making a salary stream yet it is hard to do it without any preparation. Generally you need a great deal of cash and you have to accept a ton of obligation before you can put resources into property. Stocks are close to difficult to put resources into with totally none of your own cash and you have to know a ton about the financial exchange before you start. Ordinary organizations cost a ton of cash to begin so they probably won't be your best choice.

In any case, you can make a web business without any preparation. It is okay and can really make you are great pay stream in the event that you realize what you are doing and you buckle down.

There are a couple of various approaches to profit online without any preparation, however email advertising bests the rest. It is one of the most straightforward approaches to produce an easy revenue on the web and interestingly, nearly anybody with a PC can do it.

Here is the way it works. You make a lot of consecutive messages that structure an 'email pamphlet'. You at that point get individuals to pursue your email bulletin and give you authorization to send them messages.

It tends to be done on 100% autopilot. So you compose the messages once and after that when somebody joins they are sent the messages in succession. They will get email 1 first, at that point seven days after the fact they will get email 2, at that point one more week later they will get email 3, etc.

In each email (or in only a portion of your messages) you incorporate a showcasing message that business sectors a pertinent item or administration. It may be your very own item or it may be a member item. At whatever point somebody navigates and pays for whatever item or administration you are showcasing you get a commission.

Email showcasing is very easy to do, however so as to be fruitful at it you have to instruct yourself. You have to realize how to inactively create traffic, you have to realize how to change over traffic into leads and how to change over leads into deals. Interestingly, it doesn't take long to gain proficiency with these things and anybody can learn them.

Automated revenue isn't something that was developed with the appearance of web. Yet, what the approach of web has done is to build the chances to make it. Every day an ever increasing number of individuals are exchanging over to creating easy revenue on the web. These individuals are not simply sit homemakers hoping to make some additional buck in their spare time, at the same time, are committed experts like specialists and legal counselors who are searching for approaches to enhance their pay. Things being what they are, how might you produce automated revenue on the web? There are numerous approaches to do it and it is past the extent of this article to clarify them all. Let us simply take a gander at the three most rewarding fields - independently publishing, subsidiary promoting, sites.

Indeed, even with so much discussion of data over-burden, individuals are as yet hungry for data. Data is required on a ton of points. It very well may be identified with your expert life, individual life or even your interest. You can independently publish to give out diminishes data. It very well may be as digital books, booklets, manuals, recordings, sound tapes, CDs. Explicitly for the web you can distribute digital books, articles and e-manuals. How - To books and articles are extremely well known on the web and these sell like hot cupcakes. You need to distribute, market and offer these items to profit. In this way, whatever cash that you make is all yours. You likewise have total proprietorship and control of these books. Best of all, it doesn't require any money related speculation from your part. The main venture that is required is the speculation of you exertion and imagination.

A large portion of us have found out about offshoot showcasing even before we knew about web. Items like Avon, Tupperware, and Amway and so on were showcased along these lines. The web has just expanded the capability of offshoot showcasing. It resembles owning a shopping center where you acquire cash from the benefits of the shopping center just as from the benefits earned by every individual store in your shopping center. Partner promoting on the web is so prominent on the grounds that you have such a tremendous market to advertise your items. The entire world is really your market. Associate showcasing doesn't require any speculation. The quantity of individuals working under you will choose the income you receive in return. The more the quantity of individuals, more will be your pay. The main thing you have to contribute is time and exertion. When you have built up a system you can take a load off from the salary that you make.

Going to the third choice, for example producing pay from sites. Sites are additionally called online genuine bequests. The site that you claim is your property and you make cash utilizing your site. There are numerous approaches to profit from a site yet the most significant thing to recall is that you ought to have a great deal of guests to your site to profit from it. Presently, how would you guarantee that you get a great deal of guests to your site? To get it going, you need to build your internet searcher positioning. There are numerous approaches to do this also. In this way, what do you put on your site. Indeed, it very well may be anything. It very well may be a site of your articles. It could be site given to your leisure activity like cultivating. On the off chance that the substance of your site is great individuals will return to your site. You would then be able to produce income through commercials set on your site. They can be flags or some other mode. It very well may be through compensation per snap conspires, etc. You need not be a site engineer to create one. Be that as it may, make sure to counsel one preceding you go about. In the event that you believe you can't manage the cost of it, at that point there are a lot of assets accessible online for individuals like you to experience.

Whichever sort of business you do, remember that you will require parcel of tolerance before you make this into a normal wellspring of pay. This isn't a lottery ticket. You can't simply begin making millions exactly at the snap of your fingers. This will require significant investment and tolerance previously, you go anyplace close to the pay that you are longing for.

The vast majority buckle down to bring home the bacon. Nonetheless, inquire about has demonstrated that numerous individuals are troubled at their particular employment. They would prefer to accomplish something different or be with their family. When you are exchanging your time for cash, you are really dealing with a functioning salary. Dynamic salary implies you must be effectively attempting to get paid. To have time opportunity, what you should work for is easy revenue. Easy revenue is a sort of salary stream that in the event that you to assemble it appropriately, it will pay you again and again notwithstanding when you are not physically working at it. Many individuals might want to know how they can gain easy revenue. One method for doing so is to begin an online business.

Building easy revenue streams with an online business might be out of the standard. Most money related masters will propose for you to put resources into investment properties to produce automated revenue. Property rental is a smart thought and web business can create leftover pay moreover. How does the idea work?

To start, you have to appreciate the game plan of accomplice displaying. Most of the vendors online attract accomplices or administrators for their exhibiting exertion. Accomplice elevating has been exhibited to convey better results and generously more monetarily canny. You can start a web business by essentially selecting on the merchant part program. In any case, to create computerized income on the web, you have to get together with a shipper that has participation things or organizations.

When you are the individual from a shipper that solicitations month to month participation portion, you are exceptionally the route toward structure your simple income. When you make sense of how to check a customer for the standard shipper, a section of the portion made by the customer is your reward. The merchant is granting their general income to you to help more arrangements.

In summary, it is possible to gain robotized income from the web. The test is to find the right part program that pays waiting pay. Various people has achieve time and cash related open door from following a comparative condition. The resulting stage to building your wcb business is to learn web promoting frameworks.

Budgetary pros regularly scan for authoritatively settled associations accessible to be obtained. These viably settled business associations are sold by the owners for explicit reasons. From time to time, contributing on such a standard business can be making up for the theorists while off course, insufficient appraisal can lead you to a tremendous cash related hazard. Here, you will locate some direct, phenomenal strategies for evaluating a mechanized income business accessible to be bought. In the event that you're willing to contribute on such an ebb and flow business on the web, you have to require some venture and research broadly before you overwhelm.

Bit by bit directions to survey a robotized income business accessible to be obtained: methodologies explained fundamental

#1. Examine the history and track records

This fills in as the fundamental technique for screening a present business. This methodology will empower you to shortlist a segment of the potential associations to contribute on. You have to do explore on the association and examine the history and track records. There are a couple of locales and associations offering basic appraisal organizations. You can get an expert or you can cross check these parts autonomous from any other person. Find progressively about the high focuses and depressed spots, starting endeavors, turnover, cash related cases and various records to survey the business in the basic stage.

#2. Research and check the prospects and conceivable outcomes

During this stage, you have to do the homework as the future owner of a business. You have to research the conceivable outcomes and prospects circumspectly. In this stage, you'll need to work with the benefits available on the web. You should moreover direct with the experts in the particular claim to fame to get some answers concerning the viability and the future prospects of that division. You should in like manner consider close by and worldwide prospects to choose a canny decision. A business should reliably be surveyed by its far away future prospect. If it is apparently a conventional compensation generator in future, you can proceed and counsel with the shipper.

#3. Get some answers concerning the contenders

This stage could be considered as a bit of research arrange. Regardless, researching the contenders expect a huge activity paying little mind to whether you're setting a business without any planning. You should watch the contenders eagerly for quite a while. You have to make sense of how they're proceeding with new contemplations and features. You should endeavor to have an undeniable idea with respect to the test and how much you'll have to lock in and stay before all. A computerized income business requires minute appraisal about the contenders. You have to investigate to envision the aftereffect of an endeavor.

#4. Consult with the merchant to show signs of improvement offer

In case you're persuaded about the possibility of a business available to be purchased, it's a great opportunity to arrange the cost. You need to investigate other comparable organizations available to be purchased and get a thought regarding estimating. This will enable you to make a decent proposition and estimating offer. You need to comprehend the conditions and follow up to get the best bargain.

CHAPTER FIVE

HOW TO LEVERAGE SOCIAL MEDIA FOR PASSIVE INCOME

Anybody can profit on the off chance that they're willing to place in more hours at work, yet not every person has opportunity to do it. That is the place automated revenue proves to be useful.

Profiting while you rest (truly) feels extraordinary, but at the same time it's shrewd. On the off chance that you can procure a check without a ton of work, you've set yourself up for an agreeable future. Luckily, the web is basically intended to create easy revenue — it just requires a little information and exertion.

1) Use Your Blog

In the event that you haven't just made an adapted blog, at that point start one today. It's perhaps the most ideal ways you can produce pay without a great deal of work. The extraordinary thing about a blog is that it regularly takes under 10 hours of the week to keep up, yet it can possibly make a similar income as a 40-hour work week.

Simply beginning a blog isn't sufficient to create easy revenue, however. You'll have to set up activities that will keep on working when you're nowhere to be found. Here are probably the most well known techniques:

Compose an eBook: After you've composed a few blog entries on a specific subject, it's genuinely simple to incorporate the data into an eBook, which you can sell on the web. In case you're just selling each duplicate for $0.99, and you sell 1K duplicates in a month, that is an extra $1K in your pocket.

Promote: Advertisements are the most well-known type of automated revenue for websites. Organizations will pay as much as possible to promote on your blog in the event that it gets enough traffic.

Compose Affiliate Reviews: With an offshoot connection implanted into your audit, you'll profit each time somebody taps on a connection as well as buys an item.

Accomplice Up: Another type of subsidiary connecting comes when you join forces with another organization; you can offer a coupon code for an item or administration sold on another blog. Each time somebody utilizes that coupon code, you'll get paid.

2) Make Videos

Recordings are very well known via web-based networking media today, especially now that Facebook has organized the autopay highlight. At the point when a video starts playing, most of shoppers won't click away. They'll watch the video completely.

Thus, on the off chance that you can make an extraordinary video and market it to general society, you can gain huge cash from ads. At the point when on the finance stage, YouTube will pay a couple of pennies each time somebody watches the video, which are reserves that originated from different promoters. A couple of pennies isn't much in the event that you just get a couple of hundred perspectives, however on the off chance that you get many thousands and that's just the beginning, you can make a pretty penny.

Viral recordings are likewise extraordinary for creating automated revenue. When the video is made, it will circle the web through online life and YouTube. You can profit from commercials and perspectives for a considerable length of time after a viral video courses the web.

3) Social Media Management

This doesn't remove much from your day by day timetable, and you can make a considerable amount of cash from your endeavors. Regardless of whether you're dealing with your very own social profile or assuming control over the administration for a business, there are tricky ways you can assemble some additional salary as an afterthought.

The initial step is to construct a decent after. At that point, you can share substance and connects and create a discourse about each. Organizations will pay you to share this substance on the off chance that you get enough commitment.

You can likewise interface your site to web based life on the off chance that you have items or administrations worth selling. On the off chance that shoppers appreciate the substance you share, they'll tail you back to your site, and you can take advantage of this association.

CHAPTER SIX

ABOUT RENTING, WEBSITE FLIPPING, SELLING EBOOKS AND BEING CREATIVE

Estimating, when selling digital books is relative, similarly as with some other items. What's more, on the off chance that you need to make cash selling digital books, you need to value it right in light of the fact that regardless of how astoundingly it's composed, how great the data is and how one of a kind it is, if it's not estimated right, you won't make a lot of, or any, deals.

The accompanying data will assist you with pricing your eBook right so you make deals - and maybe start fabricating your own little eBook composing and distributing domain.

Make Money Selling Ebooks: Factors Prospects Consider When Buying Ebooks

A few things to remember when attempting to peruse your clients are that they purchase dependent on various components.

A portion of these are nature of data offered, brand observation, regardless of whether they're comfortable with your items and administrations, how the topic is secured, regardless of whether there's whatever else similar available, how it's exhibited, and so forth.

The majority of this influences what you can pull off charging.

To Make Money Selling Ebooks, Price to Appeal to the Masses and Create Lifetime Customers

Numerous eBook writers value their digital books to contend with others in their specialty. New eBook distributers will in general value lower, assuming that they'll get more deals that way. Be that as it may, as my model above outlines, this isn't generally the situation. There are a lot more factors to consider, as we've talked about.

In any case, as I would like to think, this is as yet a decent model to go with. This is called evaluating to infiltrate the market, and following is the reason I believe it's a shrewd valuing system, particularly for new authors and independent publishers who need to be fruitful when they sell digital books on the web.

Sell Ebooks Online Insight: Pricing to Penetrate a Market - What This Is and Why It Works

The thought behind it is to get the same number of clients as you can with the goal that you can develop your mailing rundown and transform these one-time clients into lifetime clients by offering different items and administrations to them. This is a decent technique on the off chance that you intend to compose more digital books, make courses, sell partner items, and so forth.

Keep in mind however, there's a fine balance between evaluating to infiltrate the market and harming your image. You would prefer not to be shoddy to such an extent that your eBook has no apparent worth, however you would prefer not to be costly to the point that you don't make a decent number of offers. It's an exercise in careful control.

In any case, remember this: Once clients purchase from you once, they're significantly more liable to purchase from you once more. What's more, as indicated by the Pareto Principle, 20% of your clients will represent 80% of your eBook deals. In this way, estimating to get lifetime clients can be incredibly worthwhile.

I know. I have clients who returned and purchase from me again and again - and many even give me thoughts of items they'd like me to make. This resembles having dollars tossed at you since they're stating, "In the event that you compose it, I'll get it!"

Make Money Selling Ebooks: Want to Start an eBook Publishing Empire - Use This Pricing Strategy for Success

So in the event that you need to begin an eBook distributing domain, at that point utilizing this estimating model is an amazing procedure for guaranteeing long haul deals and a constant flow of new clients.

What I suggest on the off chance that you utilize this valuing model is to evaluate the challenge. Get highs and lows of what comparable items are selling for. At that point, go in somewhere in the center.

What's more, ensure you have an amazing deals page. This will for all intents and purposes guarantee that you make cash selling digital books - and fringe items that you may make around your eBook (eg, e-classes, extra digital books in a similar line, and so on.). Get familiar with how to compose an eBook and value it to sell.

Did you know composing and selling digital books have turned out to be one of the most beneficial 'work at home' organizations on the Internet? Composing and selling digital books can be very rewarding. Everybody searches for data on the Internet. On the off chance that you can give them the sort of data they truly need, they will be glad to pay you for it. Gain from the prosperous about eBook showcasing insider facts to guarantee you of achievement.

There are various approaches to sell millions digital books. In the event that one of your objectives is to turn into a Millionaire or make a six-figure salary online at that point consider selling digital books by the amount. The vast majority simply set an objective of making a million dollars over the Internet and that is great however most plans miss the mark regarding making that sort of salary since making cash is there just objective. At the point when your objective of having your very own home web business that has that sort of achievement of acquiring one million dollars with the accentuation on selling countless units then your prosperity will be entirely feasible.

The main thing you might need to consider is composing your very own eBook and selling it on the web. There are a lot of points on which you can compose a digital book, simply pick one that you are appropriate for. Digital books are not unreasonably hard to compose and they don't take that long to think of one. You can compose an eBook in one day. Numerous digital books are just around 25 pages. Some digital books are around 200 pages. Simply expound on something that you definitely know. Consider your occupation or the side interests that you have and you will understand that you are near a specialist regarding that matter.

In the event that you just have one eBook that you need to sell so as to make a million dollars then you should sell one million digital books making one-dollar benefit on every one. This would be probably the hardest methods for selling one million digital books. In the event that your benefit was 2 to 5 dollars on each eBook, at that point you won't need to sell the same number of to make one million dollars.

Selling a million units with only one eBook title may take a few years regardless of whether is a mainstream subject and elegantly composed that would speak to an enormous group of spectators or pull in numerous purchasers and clients. Despite the fact that it is entirely conceivable to sell one million digital books from only one title in a brief timeframe, most writers have a couple digital books to numerous digital books available to be purchased.

Your odds of selling one million digital books increment drastically when you have numerous titles that you are selling simultaneously. On the off chance that you have 30 digital books that you have composed and they are incredible digital books and advance to numerous clients then your objective of selling one million digital books will build extraordinarily and significantly more immediately then selling only one title.

Utilize your creative mind and attempt to consider having 100 to 1000 eBook titles that you could sell and to what extent it would take to sell one million digital books. You can sell other writer's digital books and make a benefit off of them, which will get you closer to your objective of selling numerous digital books up to one million digital books. Clearly the more eBook titles you have the closer you will be to your objective in selling one million digital books.

Practically you can have just 25 titles of digital books that you have composed or have obtained affiliate rights on and sell one million digital books in about a year. The key is to choose the prevalent classes on what sells best on the Internet. At that point the following thing you will need is to publicize it by utilizing an eBook portrayal that would make all individuals need to purchase your digital book. I have more data regarding this matter.

The matter of selling eBooks online can be entirely productive. Digital books are electronic books that don't require printing - is essentially a non-material item that doesn't have any expenses to create an extra duplicate. digital book can undoubtedly contain any data you need to share and think would be helpful for your clients, and it doesn't expect you to compose it. You can without much of a stretch utilize the data accessible online for nothing - gather it and reuse it in your digital book. Along these lines you can begin your own eBook business - sell them on the web and make a fortune. The matter of conveying data as bulletins or eBooks are incredibly gainful, yet for a startup adventure it is imperative to be guided to the correct heading and get moving.

You can pursue the accompanying strides to make and exceed expectations a business of selling eBooks on the web:

1. Right off the bat you have to accompany a thought of what sort of eBook you need to sell. This can be the meeting to generate new ideas. The best is compose an eBook that suits you as an individual - on a theme that is truly intriguing to you. Do you know a great deal about paragliding? Amazing. Offer your insight in a digital book. Do you realize how to profit on the web? Offer your tips - how you began on the web, how you began selling and profiting. Discover a point that looks fascinating for individuals. Generally it is on the best way to get more cash-flow, how to set

aside cash, how to spare time and lessen work endeavors. Self improvement guides additionally sell incredibly. Such subjects have consistently been mainstream with many individuals and there are numerous potential purchasers for your digital book.

2. When you have chosen the point of your digital book, at that point you should begin gathering the data or start setting up the eBook. Web has huge amounts of openly accessible data on any of the subjects. There are many sites/discussions on every specialty, so you should simply just to gather data, sort it and mastermind it in an appropriate request, record everything and there you have - some extremely incredible substance for your new digital book. On the off chance that you need more time to do it without anyone else's help, you can generally enlist an individual online on an independent site to do some work for you - gather particular sort of data, accumulate it and make it valuable for your digital book.

3. In the wake of composing or setting up the advanced substance, it must be accumulated as a book. The vast majority utilize the Word or some other comparable office type items to compose their data. Notwithstanding, composing isn't all that matters - you need a few pictures, designs on your eBook - particularly the spread. You can generally contract a structured on an independent site to plan a digital book's spread and internal pages for you.

Likewise make a point to contract editor (in case you're not a local language speaker) - to illuminate all the punctuation botches. When you have everything done all you have to do is simply to assemble your eBook into a pdf record - which is the most famous arrangement for digital books today. Once more, on the off chance that you don't have a clue how to do this, there are constantly numerous individuals that can support you.

4. The following need is the issue of showcasing the item. Presently the eBook is prepared, a legitimate structure is required for the site to advertise the item to the planned purchasers. You have to compose an attempt to seal the deal page that would sell your item. There are proficient individuals who compose such pages, so you can generally employ one on a consultants site. An appropriately planned site and extraordinary deals page will change over your guests into purchasers and it will result you in numerous deals.

5. When you have that prepared, simply get an area name under a web facilitating organization. What's more, you will have a completely working site.

6. Presently you have a working site and an incredible eBook - how to acknowledge installments? You should discover an installment processor that will acknowledge your item and enable you to process installments on the web - acknowledge charge card

and PayPal installments on the web. There are organizations that enable you to sell your computerized items on the web and acknowledge Mastercard installments from your clients. Appropriate installment techniques will give your purchasers a chance to pay for your eBook effectively and certainly pull in the purchasers for simple and advantageous shopping.

7. At that point once you have everything prepared and set up all you should do is simply to proceed to begin advancing your site. There are numerous approaches to advance your digital books site on the web - utilize accessible partner systems where you will pay associates to advance your eBook and along these lines you will acquire cash. Compose articles, fabricate connections to your site. Present your site to significant site catalogs. This will pull in intrigued guests and you will begin selling your digital book.

On fruitful fulfillment of all the above advances, you can rest guaranteed that your business would thrive and you would profit. Along these lines, on the off chance that you have some data which can be sold on the web, you can just change them into advanced data and can have a gainful business. It is anything but a simple assignment to compose a digital book, anyway there is no free cash - even on the web and there is no enchantment slug. You need to buckle down with a correct arrangement and at exactly that point you will succeed. In any case, when you succeed and start making your first deals you will be upbeat that you begun this online business.

Selling eBooks online doesn't need to be as disheartening as it shows up. Indeed, you as well, the non-specialized merchant can sell your very own eBook items online without the assistance of any outer organizations. You don't have to pay month to month charges to have your downloadable digital books sold for you. You can begin selling digital books directly from your own server.

Give me a chance to give you a diagram of how the matter of selling eBooks online works.

When clients buy an eBook on the web, they need it ASAP, similar to, at the present time! What's more, the main way most organizations that sell digital books manage this is to pay an outer online organization to enable them to give the quick conveyance of the downloadable item. The organization that they employ for this activity will make a procedure wherein the eBook item being sold is naturally made accessible for the client, upon installment.

In any case, here's the place the issue lies.

The Deception

These online organizations realize the defenselessness associated with the selling of eBook downloads. They realize a great many people aren't developers and consequently will exploit that shortcoming by establishing absurd installment designs that are woefully pointless. They are completely mindful that you need learning with regards to the functions of the back-end procedure of web programming, and therefore are helpless before their impulses. In this manner, they will charge you far too much for something they shouldn't charge you for.

Rather than having you pay only one level and last expense for selling your eBooks, they'll entice you with bright reasons about why you should keep on paying them month to month for it. Different organizations are even striking enough to take a level of each eBook deal that you make utilizing their administration, notwithstanding the regularly scheduled installments they charge. Since you don't have a clue about any better, you consider these installments or reasonings the "cost of working together" when in actuality, it isn't. It is the expense of being clueless.

The Goal and The Reality

Presently, I don't think about you, however the vast majority I know, when they go online to begin selling eBooks, they need to get however much cash-flow as could reasonably be expected. Also, in case you're similar to those different suckers who are really dishing out cash on a month to month reason for these sham sites to sell your eBook items for you, let this be an enlightening cautioning:

You Don't Have to Do That! It is a Complete Waste of Money!

Truly, I realize that some of you incline toward others to sell your eBook items for you since you have definitely no programming aptitudes or information and you favor another person to take the necessary steps for you. I get that. In any case, regardless you are being ripped off. On the off chance that you couldn't care less to spare or keep the vast majority of the price tag that a client pays for your downloadable eBook items, at that point, this eBook article is certainly NOT for you.

My Story

There was a period I use to dream about having the option to naturally sell my very own eBooks for nothing. However, in those days, it was only a fantasy, a desire, a dream. I had numerous eBooks to sell, however was disheartened by the measure of work I found was fundamental so as to get that going.

PayPal, the most confided in installment framework, tragically, doesn't give a basic route to its clients/vendors to sell eBooks (or any downloadable record besides). Also, being the incredibly bustling individual that I am, I quit any pretense of attempting to make sense of how to do it all alone. Despite everything I had the option to sell my eBooks on the web, however I had no real option except to do so physically, which was carefully tedious.

To give my clients the INSTANT eBook download that I had guaranteed them on my "Purchase Now" page, I needed to remain stuck to the PC and watch for new arranges. At the point when the new eBook requests arrived, I needed to rapidly email every client their item individually. This was unfathomably awkward, as I'm certain you would already be able to envision.

Following quite a while of doing this, I understood on the off chance that I am to keep selling digital books on the web, I would need to make sense of something else, proficient and make it free. I essentially couldn't keep on physically email my clients their eBook items any longer since deals were quickly expanding and it would have been an enormous undertaking for one individual.

I had no real option except to ponder this. I dove profound into my prepared information of programming and chose to compose my own eBook selling PHP utility. It took half a month to configuration, compose and complete the code for it yet when it was finished, it was to be sure a wondrous thing. It worked superbly. It had the option to flawlessly sell my eBooks for me without necessitating that I remained stuck to the PC.

Site FLIPPING

Site flipping is a web advertising movement that has created a ton of intrigue, and has increased progressively in the course of the most recent couple of years. As a matter of fact, it has been around any longer than a couple of years and has existed in numerous structures, anyway it is as of late that it has begun to premium a wide cross segment of advertisers, as they start to acknowledge exactly that it is so productive to flip sites for money!

How Does Site Flipping Work?

The focal idea driving site flipping is a basic one. Fundamentally, it is gaining a site and after that "flipping" or "selling" it at a benefit. Clearly, this is the same old thing and it has been accomplished for quite a long time. For instance; some time prior, Hotmail.com was offered to Microsoft for millions, and, all the more as of late, YouTube was offered to Google. Throughout the years, this has happened to various sites, these simply happen to be two of the greatest.

How Has Website Flipping Evolved?

At once, the.com fever implied that many individuals were 'flipping' spaces rather than sites. What this implied was that individuals would purchase space names that may be viewed as significant, for example, Internetmarketing.com, and afterward showcase them at premium costs. These days, stays a fundamental piece of site flipping, however nowadays, it isn't sufficient to simply sell an area name except if it's an especially decent one (at any rate, the greater part of the great names are taken or should be purchased at ultra mind-boggling expenses).

The Basic Strategy of Website flipping

At its most essential, the idea of site flipping, or selling sites at a benefit, implies that you have to persuade potential purchasers that the site you need to sell is worth more than you gotten it for. In this way, you either need to discover a site that was underestimated in any case (and afterward sell it dependent on its real worth), or you have to improve and tidy up the site you need to sell with the goal that it is more alluring than when you previously acquired it, thus can be sold at an expanded worth.

This is the troublesome piece of site flipping, and is the motivation behind why numerous individuals regularly think that its intense to do when they initially begin. On the off chance that you have no past experience building or redesigning locales, you could end up soiled down attempting to make sense of how to improve your site.

Cheer up however, as there are numerous assets out there to support you. The gatherings are loaded with individuals willing to offer guidance and data to new advertisers, if you contribute back. With a little research and study, you ought to have the option to gain proficiency with all that you need. In this way, all things considered, you may find that site flipping is possibly a very productive venture. Simply ensure you go into it with your eyes wide open, and that you are set up to take every necessary step to realize what you have to make flipping sites for benefit a suitable endeavor.

Subsequent to consuming the 12 PM oil for quite a long time and maybe months structuring your site and advancing it for traffic, it is presently time to encash your diligent work and drudge. You need to sell your site, however tragically you don't have any information of how to go about it. The procedure to purchase and sell sites for a benefit is named as Website flipping. Fundamentally site flipping word is gotten from the property business where an engineer purchases a real estate parcel, creates it and sells it at a higher worth, gaining benefit for his endeavors. Site Flipping is additionally to some degree comparative where a speculator purchases a site, improves it and sells it at a more expensive rate in this manner acquiring benefits.

Since the expense of area flipping is expanding as time passes, site flipping is a reasonable option and it is likewise inside the range of a normal speculator. Site flipping is picking up notoriety among financial specialists. This wonder can be clarified by contrasting it and property advancement. It is significantly more advantageous to buy a readymade house than developing one from a scratch. It spares a great deal of time and obviously cash, since swelling makes the value rise persistently. In a similar vein it is considerably more advantageous to purchase a built up site rather than the tedious procedure of getting every one of the apparatuses important to construct a site.

It appears to be intriguing purchase a site yet it is difficult. Purchasing a site costs a great deal of cash and for a youthful financial specialist there isn't much scope for another opportunity as the misfortunes caused in a disappointment will be generous and devastating. Accordingly before picking to purchase and sell sites ensure that you have the essential aptitude to build the estimation of the site with the goal that you can procure from site flipping benefits.

The web has hurled various open doors for business and trade. There are various sites which are progressing nicely and having a not too bad traffic. Tragically the individuals who claim these sites don't have the foggiest idea how to procure cash from their sites either because of numbness or by decision. There are a large group of potential outcomes and strategies like adapt, enhance, subsidiary and upsell for most extreme addition in benefits.

Search engine optimization systems are comprehended by a little minority of website admins and executed by a miniscule number of website admins. However, this circumstance won't keep going for long and an ever increasing number of individuals are learning SEO and structuring better sites. In this manner now is the ideal opportunity to snatch this business opportunity. All it needs is a little information about SEO, a will to investigation and buckle down and a smidgen of cash to purchase sites and there is heaps of cash which can be made as benefits.

The Steps associated with Website Flipping:

• Before attempting to purchase and sell sites it would be a relevant inquiry to pose How will you set a cost for your site? The diverse variable which can impact the cost of a site incorporates the work in question, various instruments and specialized aptitudes which are essential for keeping up the site, sundry costs like facilitating, showcasing, staff, and so forth, development of business and potential for future development.

• While choosing a site it is imperative to pick the right site which has extent of progress.

• While you select a site, pick one which sells the item or administrations which you as of now produce or sell. It will give you numerous extra advantages like guiding the traffic of the site to your items or administrations.

• Choose locales which have awesome substance however has been ineffectively upgraded. In the wake of acquiring the rights for the site you can improve by republishing the substance or do some article advertising.

• A website which has a discussion with an enormous group of spectators or clients is a goldmine for an ambitious web business person. Such locales could be controlled by specialists who don't have the foggiest idea how to improve or adapt the site. One can purchase such destinations and it will cost a minor sum when contrasted with the procuring potential it will have. This is one of the most firmly protected site flipping mysteries.

• After choosing a site you should expand the estimation of the site. The estimation of a site can be expanded by improving traffic and page rank by certain SEO methods. This will ensure an expansion in benefits.

• While selling a site it is smarter to sell it at a similar spot where you got it. Any improvement in estimation of the site will be founded on similar criteria which decided its worth.

Site flipping has tremendous advantages when contrasted with different types of speculation like property and space venture. Capital inclusion is the barest least and enables another web financial specialist to enter the market. Most venture is dormant as for increment in worth while site flipping course includes an expansion in incentive by reasonable upgrades.

Site Flipping can be partitioned into three structures:-

• The amateur's flipping-It includes building up a site from the earliest starting point, advancing it and selling it for benefit after it starts creating a not too bad benefit. Despite the fact that it is a tedious procedure it gives better control, arrangement and the intrigue zone of the site.

• Standard Flipping-This is the most widely recognized type of flipping and includes the purchasing of a nice site and expanding its worth rapidly and afterward selling it for a benefit.

• Long Term Investment Flipping-It includes purchasing a site which is giving a customary pay and taking measures with the goal that the worth is kept up and the salary is constantly produced. It requires more noteworthy capital and a ton of persistence and time.

The present situation of Website flipping business is splendid and is the quickest developing on the web showcase. The market existed before yet just of since it has discovered significance.

Since the costs engaged with area flipping are gigantic Website flipping is a simpler and practical choice. Also the significant lot it takes to structure and make another site. In this way on the off chance that you are knowledgeable in the specialty of SEO it will be smarter to purchase a site and enhance it with great SEO methodologies like including content, fixing title labels, and connecting structure, article advertising and so on.

Numerous individuals use site turning to gain a smidgen of salary to a great extent as an afterthought. It truly is perfect for that as a couple of hours work could really net you a couple of hundred dollars - on the off chance that you recognize what you're doing. Be that as it may, some go a stage well beyond this and begin to transform their site flipping endeavors into a genuine business. Thusly, they furnish themselves with a quite decent constant flow of pay!

Essentially, the thought behind maintaining a site flipping business truly isn't too convoluted. All that it means is that you will flip sites consistently with the goal that you win a constant flow of salary. Going about site flipping as such anyway implies that you can utilize different systems at different occasions so as to accomplish some incredible outcomes.

Because you're flipping sites does not imply that you have to get done with flipping one site before you start on another. That is a confusion among numerous who flip sites on low maintenance premise. In all honesty, you should know at this point certain upgrades (especially those including traffic) set aside some effort to 'kick in', and once you've improved a specific site you can bear to pause and let things that impact while you proceed onward to the following site.

Thusly, you'll have the option to ceaselessly thought of a surge of sites that you can auction. Additionally, you'll need to opportunity to return and assess your choices by and by just on the off chance that you feel a specific site could be improved further in specific ways. Dealing with different sites as such can be confounding now and again, which is the reason it is basic for anybody running a site turning to be amazingly sorted out.

Toward the day's end, you'll see that there truly is a ton to pick up by consistently flipping sites in this style. Since you're concentrating on flipping sites constantly, as opposed to just giving a brief period to a great extent to it, you'll see that you can be extra adaptable. For instance, you could purchase and improve 5 sites in a day, and after that let them sit tight for 3 months before you sell them. Meanwhile, you could likewise every now and then auction certain sites in the event that you need some additional money to a great extent.

On the off chance that you realize how to make extraordinary looking sites that perform, you might be equipped for taking in substantial income by site flipping. Site flipping isn't not normal for house flipping in unmistakable domain. With house flipping, you place cash directly into a fixer-upper and you at that point sell the as good as ever house for a benefit. Similar works with virtual land. At whatever point you make a site and you're in a situation to adapt this site to guarantee that it's a completely working web business, there are numerous individuals who might be set up to compensation as much as possible for such a thing. There are numerous individuals in this world who're confused with regards to web composition and coding it's a sure thing without fail; in case you're satisfactory, that is.

Making a Site

The main thing you have to do before you start building destinations with the goal of webpage flipping is to purchase online to find mainstream patterns right now. There are a couple of destinations which are structured carefully for site flipping. By setting off to these sites you can see what sorts of destinations are being offered, what the different locales do, how much those destinations make on an every day/week by week/month to month premise, and so on. These sites can run anyplace from some measure of cash right as much as $2000 or progressively, in view of a few elements.

A few angles that could change the cost include:

The site style, illustrations, and so forth. How incredible the site looks, essentially.

The usefulness of the site. Precisely what does it do?

How a lot of cash the site makes on auto-pilot. (AdSense income, enrollment site, and so on.)

How hot the specialty or sort of site is right then and there.

The age of the site, how settled it is, and so on.

And that's just the beginning...

By seeing what's on offer, you can comprehend what locales to concentrate on.

Top Sellers

It's additionally insightful to investigate what destinations have as of late been sold. Most site flipping sites give a space to as of late sold sites. This will tell you what people are set up to compensation for the different destinations and specialties accessible. This truly is extraordinary information to utilize in your very own site flipping business.

Selling Websites

On the off chance that you are another comer to the organization of site flipping, you may have a little trouble getting people to confide in you. You can by making a profile about the different webpage flipping sites that is amazingly straightforward. Utilize claim photograph and let individuals know however much as could be expected about what your identity is and what you are attempting to do. At that point, make sites that have all the earmarks of being incredible and that capacity delightfully. Additionally, endeavor to cling to the locales on the off chance that you can. Endeavor to age them a little and attempt to get the different destinations built up. These sorts of sites will constantly empower you to get more salary eventually.

The cruel truth when site flipping is that you are pondering making a 'business inside a crate' basically. Most businessmen are searching for a site that they can simply transfer to their server and go. That is the thing that you will need to give. You can make a ton of cash flipping locales in the event that you look for data and you figure out how to make sites that individuals are intrigued and pay incredible cash for.

HOW TO MAKE MONEY ONLINE NOW

21 ideas to work and earn money from wherever you want with Trading Bitcoin and Forex, Blogger, Web Development, Creating Animation Video

DIEGO DE GIOVANNI

information is without contract or any type of guarantee assurance.

The trademarks that are used are without any consent, and the publication of the trademark is without permission or backing by the trademark owner.

All trademarks and brands within this book are for clarifying purposes only and are the owned by the owners themselves, not affiliated with this document.

L'indice è vuoto perché non stai utilizzando gli stili paragrafo che hai scelto di visualizzarvi.

INTRODUCTION

I might initially want to thank you for setting aside the effort to peruse this instructional kindle book – you won't be disillusioned. This digital book has been composed for individuals wherever to exploit and has not been composed for others to benefit from. So, if you don't mind don't hesitate to impart it to loved ones, however kindly don't sell it onto others.

Regardless you are a busy mother, a stay at home father, a college student, or just want to earn some extra money with your spare time – doing some extra work can help you make some nice money from home.

A quick internet research can reveal many to do work from home scams. They charge you upfront high fees and lure you to work with them.

"But actually, they are just cheating you out of your hard-earned money".

What you should already have (as a minimum)

This is not rocket science and it's quite self-explanatory, but it's worth saying nevertheless. To be able to utilize these methods, you will need the following:

1. Computer or Laptop

2. An internet connection

3. Bank account

3. Spare Time

Who would benefit from this?

Everyone! Whether you're a stay at home parent or you work from home, or you are a student – many of these proven methods are a great way to earn some extra cash and will help you to save some money

CHAPTER 1
EARN MONEY FROM SKILLS

✶ 3 Different Way to Earn quick money from home.

There are many ways to earn money online, but we are going to highlight 3 Major Categories from which you can find the best way to earn money from home

1: Required Skills to do some Jobs/Projects.

2: Simple To do Tasks / Virtual Assistance.

3: Invest and Earn Profits

So, to be honest, these are the Major Ways to Earn money but hey wait let me elaborate you the sub ways under these categories from which you can really pick the best skill to work on ant get yourself ready for the opportunities that might come near soon and knock your luck door.

✶ Required Skills to do some Jobs/Projects.

✶ Graphics Design
I bet you've been there:

Sitting at a customer's concise, understanding that the plan you're going to do is dull and needs validness. Be that as it may, if that is the thing that the customer needs... you should set your desire aside and adhere to the guidelines.

Here's the thing !!!

Continually following the guidelines doesn't help on the off chance that you need to demonstrate your innovative side, adapt new methods and fabricate a stand-apart portfolio. It doesn't give you much opportunity and space for experimentation. For imaginative craftsmen, that is torment!

The uplifting news is:

To profit as a visual creator, you don't generally need to tail another person's vision. There are a lot of easy revenue openings that would enable you to plan what you need, the manner to create and abstract ideas from yours own,

Here are some skills on which you can work on and grow into your creativity

- comics and graphic novels

- coloring books

- web icons and custom illustrations

- fonts

- social media images and icon packs

- emojis and stickers

- printable wall art

Logo Design

Logo designing is used to specify a brand or an organization name. Today's business strategy has changed in more amount than before. To get maximum benefits, we must have to establish our presence online. And to create our existence on the Internet of People, to establish our Vision or a brand "Our Company's Logo" is most essential.

So this necessity could become your job opportunity, if you have talent, have a creative mind and have a skill on designing software like adobe Photoshop then you are most eligible person to earn massive income online.

Actually logo designing is most critical issue. If you managed it properly then success is yours!

Here are some tips to Create Logo Design, the steps you need to follow are as follows:-

Before going through these tips you should aware from how to use Photoshop.

- First you can create a rough design on a paper if you are full-fledged with your drawing skills or you can start creating on Photoshop.

- In Photoshop you need to work on document for which you need to take a custom size paper of width 5 inches, height 5 inches and resolution of 300 pixels.

•You can either take RGB mode or CMYK as it both will function accordingly but to view a clear image CMYK is considered to be better as RGB creates pixels and gets blur if you zoom your image.

•To create a logo you can make the use of pen tool or you can take brush tool but pen tool creates better sharp design. For pen tool you have to work on path and a layer in which you can start creating design.

•You must see to it that every design you have created, has its own layer and path. If correction needed you can select its path and by clicking Alt button you can work accordingly to it.

•After creating design in your path it will ask you for selecting and then you need to right click on path and say make selection to add color to it.

•You can also increase the size by CTRL+T. Also you can create a duplicate layer if you need the same design but you need to flip it by right clicking and say Flip horizontal or vertical you can make use of other options too i.e. Scale, Rotate, Skew, Perspective, Warp etc.

•If you want to add on some effects to your logo you can make use of blending options and accordingly make use of it usually we apply "Stroke Option" to it.

•You can also make use of Hue/Saturation, Color balance, brightness/contrast to make color changes. This option you will find in Photoshop software (Image -> Adjustments.)

•After all these steps followed you have to save the file in PSD and JPEG format and if changes required you can accordingly work on PSD file.

Adobe Photoshop Skills

•Adobe Photoshop is another trending tool where you can work on some photo editing work and earn some good amount form it, So the solution is you need to join the Adobe Photoshop Online Course. To choose the best online selling course you have to research little about high demanding skills. What are the highest demanding and highest paid graphics designing skills out there? Once you spend some money on learning graphics designing or adobe photoshop expert skills, it will make you responsible to get the return within profit. and for that, you must need to pay for the adobe photoshop course. And it's your investment.

•Once you spend some money on learning graphics designing or adobe photoshop expert skills, it will make you responsible and serious to get a return within profit. There are two advantages of online adobe photoshop course to earn money is that you will get complete details and premium stuff about the course before you join. 2nd you will get the knowledge about professional adobe photoshop skills.

•The second method is to join any offline course out there on Udemy or YouTube. Find out the top-quality people and institution in your city known as an expert in adobe photoshop. At the same time at home, you should use your time watching adobe photoshop tutorials and practicing on all those on you spare time.

•Now you got the lessons on how to use and design and edit your imagination power in Adobe Photoshop. But it's not finished yet, it's a start. So to become expert practice more and more until you really become an "Expert". Practice will increase your speed to complete the designing and editing tasks in a very quick pace of time. It will increase the accuracy and identify creativity, and perfection into your work.

T-Shirt Design

A T-shirt design that works out in color, text, slogan or some promotion about any product etc., is the one that people want to buy. The design must be Attractive with a unique idea. It requires a careful selection of some elements such as colors and text etc.

After you brainstorm and designed a brilliant T-shirt, you have to acquire some marketing skills to sell your work. Knowing some marketing selling strategies is critical if you are a getting started with freelance designer Career. There is some potential for the growth of your small T-shirt selling brand, you have to market it well. So, both the designing and marketing aspects should be handled properly into. If you do that, your chances for the growth of your brand would be higher.

Some people who consider t-shirt designing as a hobby & make millions of dollars. You can also sell your creative T-shirt design and sell them successfully with Good marketing skills

✱ Here Is how you can Sell T-Shirt Designs Online

01. Work on Unique T-Shirt Design Idea

The initial step to take for selling T-shirt plans is to have an incredible structure thought. Without an exceptional thought, it will be progressively hard to persuade customers or clients to purchase the shirts. All things considered, they are purchasing the structure and not the T-shirt.

What it means is that T-shirt as clothing are bounty in business sectors. They can buy any of these easygoing wears. Along these lines, they are probably going to settle on the T-shirt that has an awesome structure on it.

In this way, make it sure that your T-shirt plan thought is remarkable and appealing. It must discover the generally faltering consideration of individuals immediately from the start. That is the way to sell the shirts. Without any such thought, don't consider becoming wildly successful in the business department.

02. Brainstorming

The most ideal approach to get a shirt structure thought is to conceptualize. Plunk down with your group to discover which thought will sell. You have numerous alternatives. You can make sharp quips, charming plans, or have roar with laughter jokes that everyone adores. Individuals like to wear such T-shirts.

Another choice is to simply investigate the thoughts in regards to films and prevalent TV serials, without infringing their copyrights. You can likewise misuse some social side of individuals. Ensure that you have an extraordinary plan thought when you sell your craft structure to the intended interest group.

03. Learn To Design

In case you are not a designer and still want to sell T-shirt designs as your business, you should acquire some working knowledge of designs. Learn about typography and colors and how to make a good choice. Learn also how to use Adobe Photoshop. This software will help you create graphics easily.

You can also have a good experience of using clipart and word shapes. It will be useful in enhancing your image on the shirts. Also, use new apps like Word swag and Over to have some mastery over design. Get some design tips as well from online experts.

If designing is not your forte, hire a freelance graphic designer to do the job for you. In that case, you can then focus on increasing your sales.

Either you design it yourself as a freelancer, or hire a designer, make it doubly sure that the design is unique. Every element of fonts, words, clipart, images, etc. should make an impression.

04. Here Are Some Of The Printing And Selling Sites

• Merch By Amazon

Merchandise by Amazon is an extraordinary stage to sell your T-shirt plans on the web. One of the upsides of this site is its high traffic volume. As indicated by a gauge, Amazon gets around 669 million guests for each month.

This far more noteworthy than joined traffic gotten by numerous different destinations, for example, Teespring, Zazzle, CafePress, and so forth. In this way, gain admittance to those a large number of individuals a large number of whom you can transform into clients of your custom shirt.

You will get extra selling assets apparatuses at Amazon. You can utilize these apparatuses to dissect your traffic to have an understanding into dealing with the business appropriately.

• CafePress And Zazzle

Both these locales are prevalent for their simplicity of information exchange and item arrangement. These locales set the cost of printing your T-shirt plan. They likewise let you pick your sovereignty which is added to the shirt's base cost.

At Zazzle and CafePress the base costs are appealing. They likewise give you an exhibition reward. You can likewise get to a shirt creator apparatus to make your own plan before selling it from these destinations.

• Redbubble

With Redbubble, you can set up your store to sell the printed T-shirts. The site will choose the base cost. In any case, you are permitted to decide your markup.

• Shopify

Simply set up a shop at Shopify and you have fast access to a printer just as a drop shipper. You would then be able to deal with the correct harmony between your cost and different choices.

Truth be told, there are numerous other extraordinary shirts printing locales, for example, Custom Ink, Spreadshirt, Teespring, Printful, Vistaprint, UberPrints, and Print Aura. Contrast these locales with discover which one enables you to set your costs higher, other than printing your shirts on schedule. Most such destinations will likewise give you shirt producer instrument to structure the clothing without anyone else.

05. Make a Marketing Strategy

After you have a shocking structure thought and opened a retail facade or made a site to sell the plan, it is currently an opportunity to advertise it. Indeed, advertising is a pivotal stage. It can represent the moment of truth your business. Showcasing

is tied in with concocting novel approaches to contact the intended interest group. It needs a sound methodology.

Since you mean to sell T-shirt structures on the web, it naturally brings the SEO best practices to mind. Site design improvement is tied in with expediting your retail facade or site the top list items. At the point when potential clients type catchphrases identified with your business, your site must be obvious on the top indexed lists that you can guarantee by the correct enhancement procedures.

Showcasing likewise implies that you have to make sense of your objective client. Who is the one that is well on the way to purchase your T-shirt? You make a structure. Be that as it may, which age-gathering and social or instructive foundations your clients originate from?

Discover your optimal client and afterward make an arrangement to sell your T-shirt to that crowd. Try not to attempt to offer to everybody.

You will likewise be searching for influencers who can discuss your T-shirt plans on the web. They can enable you to help your business hugely. This is on the grounds that they have a huge number of supporters who will come to think about your business. Influencer showcasing is likewise an extraordinary method to assemble your image personality.

At that point, you ought to likewise investigate the advertising openings via web-based networking media. Open records on various social channels like Facebook and Twitter. At that point, normally post your substance about your one of a kind T-shirts to draw in purchasers.

These are the key focuses to consider while selling T-shirt structures on the web. Deal with every one of the angles well by contributing your time and cash cautiously.

✱ Make Money From Web Development

This is also another best approach to build your skills first and then make some sample websites to test your skills and show them to random people for feedback, if people really like your Web development work then you are good to go with this skill,

But your question how to make out from it? Well now we will discuss all about web development and how you can make a website and earn money from it!

Step:1 How to build a portfolio like a professional?

You have to have a site and a point of arrival. On the off chance that you are in the web planning industry, you should realize what I'm trying to say.

You should be obvious to the general population. You should be known and permit to be come to on any stage, whenever of the day.

The way toward making a site is simple. What's next is intense!

You have to have a straightforward web composition that feature what your identity is and what's in for the potential customer.

Regarding proportion, you should share 10% of the substance on 'about you' and the equalization 90% about the customer. You know, the reasons why they have to try and take a gander at your profile.

Step 2: Using the right tools for web design

How to begin website architecture as a tenderfoot? The stunt is by utilizing the correct instruments.

A website specialist regularly have a wide scope of devices available to them however in the event that you are a finished learner (imagining that web planning can win you cash), at that point you just need a couple of devices to begin.

Those tools are:

⟩ Turnkey and expert subjects

⟩ Page manufacturer

⟩ Web facilitating

Indeed, you just need the over three to begin with website specialist as a novice.

Select the right professional themes

This is very mission-critical. You need to have a wide range of good themes to help you kick-start some of your web design gigs.

Choosing the right themes is very important when is comes to building a good career because it will either turn on or turn off your potential clients. So, make sure you are mindful of this.

When it comes to the professional WordPress themes, for developing I recommend you to start small — this means that while it is always good to have at least 50 custom themes in your toolbox, you can start with a small figure (anywhere between 5 to 10).
These professional themes must be easy to configure, and it is almost an important requirement to have a drag and drop feature.

"You don't have much coding skill, remember?"

Why is it important to choose the right themes?

For starters, it needs to be easy to use because you have limited skills as a fresh web designer. More importantly, you don't need to get your hands dirty with the coding and all those mind bogging stuffs.
Secondly, the license would need to allow you to use it without limit (unlimited usage). You wouldn't want to buy a theme each time when you get a new client because it is going to eat away your earnings very quick.

Make Yourself Available Every time

Your customers need to realize that you exist. On the off chance that potential customers don't have any acquaintance with you exist, your work will be somewhat harder. Chances are; however, you are associated with a bigger number of individuals than you might suspect. It's essential to begin with those individuals and let them realize that you are currently accessible to construct sites.

I made my accessibility known on my own site if you mean to assemble sites for other people, you do need to have your own). I messaged people I'd done work for previously and let them realize I was accessible once more. I augmented my current systems administration associations, and, out of that, I started to arrange the initial couple of tasks.

If you haven't had any experience building sites, that is alright. We need to begin some place and I can't think about a superior time than the present moment. Figure out how to get your first web advancement customer.

Use the Right Platform

To make solid $5000+ a month as a part-time, you're going to need to be very quick and fast. If you don't really know how to build websites from scratch, now isn't the time to learn. If you *do* know how to build websites from scratch, I highly recommend that you set that knowledge aside for now. You need to use a platform.

WordPress is my favorite and I recommend it highly. It has a proven track record, open source development team behind it, community support, diverse theme options, and momentum.

Go out buy any books on web development (yet), enroll in any classes at your local college (it's a fast class and someone passionate is teaching it). You need to focus on getting results as efficiently and as effectively as possible. There has never been a better time than right now to make use of a platform that's already been built, and is well past the tipping point of quality and popularity.

If there are particular tasks that are not a part of your core strengths, consider finding a freelancer to help you with those and get yourself more polished for the competition in web development.

Charge the Right Price

If you're going to make Solid $5000+ per month, you can not be building websites for only a few hundred dollars. You're doing yourself and your clients a disservice. You need to have a open mind and charge a fair price. Consider the value that you're able to provide by leveraging a platform and by helping them put that platform to use.

If you're going to make $5000+ a month, you can't be building websites for only a few bucks,

Wrap your mind around the value time and focus on what building a website can do for your client's business. I recommend you charge $2500 per project. Don't go for less than $1000 on per project and make sure that you can finish the project with an average of over $75/hour or before deadline (that's what it takes to make $5000+ a month working part-time).

Master Your Skill Craft

As you begin to develop a traction and good experience, it's very important to invest in your time, value, education and focus on mastering your skill craft. Now is the time to start reading books and blogs on web development. Enroll in some premium online courses. Pick an area or specific skill to specialize and begin to focus on developing your skill set further into that area.

Attend events in your area of interest and network with others strong people. Ask the right questions and learn from the experience of those who've gone before you into those skills. As the demand for websites grows, so will the number of people trying to meet that demand. If you are going to stand out, you need to constantly work towards a mastery of what you do and what you work for.

As your success allows you time to sit back, go ahead and enjoy a short rest, then get right back to it and work continually towards mastery of your skills.

✴ Build a Mobile App That Actually Makes Money

Why do you want to build an app?

Mobile applications are a great way for business owners to make improvements to their company. They are also the perfect platform if you think that your idea will be the next big hit, like Instagram or Snapchat. Regardless of your reason for creating an app, I'm sure you have something in common with other prospective developers. All of you want to make money. First of all, I commend you for doing the research before you get started building your first app. I've seen so many people who were naive enough to think that just because they created an app, it would automatically generate money. That's not true. Here's an analogy. If you start a new business, will it automatically make money? Absolutely not .Fortunately, you've come to the right place. As an expert in the mobile application industry, I have the knowledge and experience to help steer you in the right direction. 90% of time spent on mobile devices is in apps. Build a profitable mobile app in less time and at a lower cost than traditional solutions with Build Fire Consumers clearly love to use apps, so the opportunity is there. The key is finding out how to choose the perfect app that will peak user interest and ultimately get downloads. But you need to realize that downloads alone don't always directly translate to dollars. Building an app is expensive, and you'll come across hidden development costs along the way. So before you dump all of your money into your new idea, you've got to make sure it will generate a profit.

Here's what you need to know.

Purchasing something in-app vs a mobile site

For those of you who already have an existing business, I'm going to assume that your company has a website. Hopefully (for your sake) that site has been optimized for mobile devices. Websites that aren't mobile friendly will turn visitors away, so if that's not something you've done, it needs to be a priority.

Now, let's discuss the customer experience and how it relates to their purchasing habits. Do you think users prefer buying on a mobile site or directly through a mobile application?

Apps wins. Here's why.

Convenience was the number one answer from respondents.

The other top responses also mirror convenience and enhance user satisfaction.

Your customers want everything fast. As I said earlier, if your website isn't optimized for mobile devices, speed can be an issue. But that's not a problem when people navigate through your app. Think of your app like any other business. The easiest way to make money is by keeping the customers happy and keep them coming back. In addition to speed and convenience, the checkout process on a mobile purchase is also much simpler. Purchases on an app get charged directly to the customer's credit card associated with their Google Play or App Store account.

Look how easy it is to buy something within an app if your customers have Apple Pay linked to their devices.

One click and done. It's that easy for the customer and you start getting money instantly. How does this compare to a mobile site? We've already established that speed is a factor, but for argument's sake, let's say your mobile site already runs fast too. What else could slow the customer down? They won't have their cards or accounts linked to your mobile site, so they'll have to input all of their information. The customer has to log in to their PayPal account or enter their credit card information. Overall, it's just a longer process and more of a headache for the user. Plus, typing out all of that information on a small screen leaves room for errors that can slow things down even more. Don't get me wrong. I'm not saying your mobile site shouldn't have a checkout page or have ways to generate money through credit card purchases. All I'm trying to do is emphasize that *in-app purchases are better*.

The platform that you launch your app on matters too. Take a look at the difference between the iOS and Android purchases.

The average purchase per user on iOS platforms are more than double Android's.

That doesn't mean that you should choose one over another. While iOS may have a higher number for the average purchase, Android dominates in terms of total users. Looking back at fourth-quarter smartphone sales last year, there were 432 million devices sold. Of the

432 million phones, 77 million had iOS software while 352 million ran on Android's platform. The two platforms combined for 99% of the market share, but Android alone accounts for 81.7%.With that said, 16% of Android developers earn over $5,000 per month with their mobile apps, and 25% of iOS developers make over $5,000 through app earnings. So keep these figures in mind if you're only planning to release on just one operating system.

What if you are selling physical products?

We briefly touched on this earlier, but I wanted to continue to elaborate on this topic. To successfully sell products through an app, you've got to put yourself in the minds of a mobile shopper.

40% of mobile users have bought something online with their smartphone.
This number continues to grow each year.
There are generational trends too. For example, Millennials dominate this category.
63% of Millennials have used smartphones and tablets to make a purchase.
I'm going to show you an example of a company that knows how to use their mobile app to drive sales and make money. You can follow their lead and apply their strategies to your app if you're selling a physical product as well. I'm referring to the company, Touch of Modern. 70% of the company's total sales are generated from mobile devices. Roughly two-thirds of those sales come directly from their app. So how do they do it Roughly 150,000 to 200,000 users download this app each month.57% of their shoppers are repeat customers. When you have the ability to focus on customer acquisition and customer retention at

the same time, it's a formula for success. It's their checkout flow that makes Touch of Modern so successful.

When you download the app, you'll create a profile that securely saves your information That way whenever customers open the app, they can get straight to shopping.

Here's how it looks.

It's a simple navigation screen. Customers can easily search for and scroll through items that they're interested in. Once they find something that peaks their interest, they can click on the product to find out more information. C Now the user will see a detailed description of the product in addition to a larger photo. If they like what they see and read, they can add it to their shopping cart with just one click.

Once it's in their cart, the customer can checkout in just one simple click.

That's it. Their app allows users to complete the shopping and purchase process in just three steps. There's way less friction here compared to a mobile ecommerce site. Plus, Touch of Modern can communicate with their customers better from the mobile app. They send app users notifications with daily deals and discounted items to encourage more purchases. Ultimately, this strategy works. If you're currently selling products on your website and mobile site, you can generate more revenue by successfully building a mobile app.

Build a profitable mobile app in less time and at a lower cost than traditional solutions with Build Fire

Free apps vs paid apps

Something else you'll want to consider is whether you're going to charge users to download your app. On average,

you would obviously generate a higher revenue per download. It may seem like a nice way to get some up-front profits, but you might turn people away if they have to pay.90% of the apps on the Apple App Store are free. But that doesn't mean you have to go that route. Paid apps are a great way to get more loyal customers. If they are willing to make the initial purchase just for installation, they may be more likely to use it and make additional purchases. However, if you're an established brand that already has retail channels and existing customers (like Touch of Modern), it's probably in your best interest to offer your app for free. People download those apps so they can save money and receive discounts, not spend more money just to have the option of shopping.
Keep in mind; your app will also have competition. So customers realize that they can find something similar and potentially better for free, rather than paying to download yours.

With free apps, you may get significantly more downloads, but the users could be less engaged. If they don't pay, there's no commitment. They could potentially download your app, check it out once and never use it again. While they may sound discouraging, you shouldn't look at it that way. It doesn't cost you anything to have users download your app and never use it. Sure, you'd prefer active users, but at the end of the day, it's not going to be detrimental to your company.
If you're on the fence about releasing a free or paid app, I'd lean towards recommending a free download. It will increase the chances of getting more downloads, and you can make money through other sources.
Here's a look at some global averages based on the CPM for different mobile app advertisements.

So there's definitely some money to be made here if you can sell advertising space on your app. Keep in mind, these numbers are just averages, and they aren't set in stone. If you have tons of active daily users and your app grows in popularity, you can negotiate a higher rate from advertisers based on those numbers.

Another way to generate money from a free app is with upgrades and subscriptions. Users can download the app for free and use the basic functions.

Then you can offer premium content or functions based on a monthly subscription.

Let's look at how a popular dating app accomplishes this on their platform.

I'm sure you've heard of Tinder. The concept is super simple. Users create a profile and add photos of themselves. Based on their location and preferences, they'll see photos of other users who match their search criteria (age, gender, etc.).

If they like another user's profile, they swipe right. If they don't, they swipe left.

When two people both swipe right on each other, they get connected and can start a conversation. Everyone who downloads this app has access to these features for free. But there are certain restrictions. If users swipe right on too many profiles in a day, they can't continue searching for 24 hours.

That's where a premium subscription comes in play. If users want to have unlimited likes, they can upgrade their account. The upgraded subscription comes with other bonus features like a location change, rewinds, and an experience without advertisements. You can apply this same business model to your app to make money. Let users download and use the app for free, but withhold the best features for users who are willing to pay.

Conclusion

Not all apps make money. If your plan is to just build one without a strategy and just sit back to collect your money, you'll be in for a rude awakening. Like a business, you need to have a strategy and goal before you start building an app. Mobile user prefer apps compared to mobile sites. So while your company definitely needs a website that's optimized for mobile devices, an app can make the customer experience much better. Sure, you'll have some upfront costs when you build, develop, and launch your app. But you can save time and money by creating an app through the Build Fire platform. If you're selling a physical product, having a mobile app will help you generate more money.

✱ Earn Money from Video and Animation

Make Money Editing Videos: 5 Websites that Pay

Video editing is the arrangement and manipulation of video shots. Simply put its an artistic and technical skill that requires adding special effects, structuring and more to videos. In this guide we will be sharing 5 websites where you can make money editing videos. The video industry nowadays is booming, with more and more people requiring professional help to create quality video content. So if you are already good at this then hold on, we have something big for you this time!

Being a freelance video editor can be demanding but equally rewarding. And even if you aren't a professional, just by having the right video editing software and some skill set you can start earning good money.

Video editing is the course of action and control of video shots. Just put its a masterful and specialized aptitude that requires including enhancements, organizing and more to recordings. In this guide we will share 5 sites where you can profit editing recordings. The video business these days is blasting, with an ever increasing number of individuals requiring proficient assistance to make quality video content. So on the off chance that you are as of now great at this, at that point hang tight, we have something important for you this time!

Being an independent video editorial manager can be requesting yet similarly fulfilling. What's more, regardless of whether you aren't an expert, just by having the correct video editing programming and some range of abilities you can begin winning great cash.

Websites that pay you for Video Editing Skills:

Viedit is an extraordinary stage for independent video editors. This stage enlists a wide range of editors, artists, and videographers. Consultants can make business recordings, internet-based life cuts, home recordings, travel films and that's only the tip of the iceberg. At whatever point a customer posts an undertaking, specialists can see these ventures and send recommendations with their own proposed cost for it. When the customer acknowledges your proposition, they pay the concurred measure of cash to ViEdit. When the video is finished and acknowledged, Viedit will discharge the installment.

As VidEdit has consultants and customers from 100 unique nations, the organization pays its specialists through generally all installment mediums e.g **PayPal, Bank Transfer, Credit** Card and the sky is the limit from there. The organization charges an expense of 5-15% from the complete installment to the consultant, contingent upon the sort of video mentioned.

MOFILM is a UK based substance maker organization. The organization makes video content for different organizations and brands. Video editors from everywhere throughout the world can pitch video thoughts or make recordings trying to win cash from intrigued brands.

On the off chance that you want to contend with the best, at that point register yourself on their site. On the off chance that you fit the necessities for a undertaking, an organization delegate will connect with you.

The organization pays its consultants through Bank move. The installment sum will fluctuate from venture to extend, so there's no standard charge to it. The organization will pay the consultant half of the sum forthright and the other half will be paid once the alters are finished.

1.Uscreen

Uscreen is a video on interest (VOD) stage and a specialist co-op that empowers people and organizations to sell recordings on the web. So on the off chance that you are a videographer or proofreader, the organization encourages you make your very own video selling stage. You can sell singular recordings or offer paid memberships. Through this stage, you can sell your recordings at any value you want, you will be the proprietor of your own store.

Uscreen has various installment choices you can get installment from your clients. These installment doors incorporate, PayPal, Stripe and Braintree. As a byproduct of facilitating you video store, Uscreen charges a little expense for every month, going from $99-388 relying upon the quantity of supporters you need for your recordings.

2. Tongal

Tongal is another incredible video content creation stage committed to making recordings for a wide range of computerized stages. They enlist a wide range of scholars, illustrators, videographers and editors. The organization capacities as rivalry site, where a video venture is posted with the prize subtleties. The consultants would then be able to pitch their thoughts through storyboarding and so on. When chosen for your pitch, the film cause will to get financing for the video. When the last alters are done, you will get paid by the organization.

Tongal pays its victors through four installment portals including, PayPal, Direct Deposit, Wire Transfer and Check. The prize cash will change from undertaking to extend so there is no standard sum that is paid.

✦ Create Your Video Content

1. Upload Your Videos To YouTube

This is presumably the most widely recognized way that most video business visionaries start to begin profiting with recordings. It's drop-dead easy to do and doesn't require a huge interest in video gear to begin:

1.   *Create a channel on YouTube*

2.   *Start transferring recordings to your channel routinely.*

When you begin to gather watchers and you begin to construct the quantity of supporters of your channel, you can join to adapt your recordings by permitting YouTube to show promotions on your recordings. The more perspectives your recordings get, the more cash that you will procure from the individuals who view or snap on your video promotions. You can begin a YouTube channel today however profit will take an extended period of time to work after some time except if you figure out how to strike gold and make a viral video immediately. There are different approaches to profit with your YouTube channel too, however, which we detail in different articles here on Video Entrepreneur Magazine:

2. Produce Videos or Offer A Video Related Service to Others

There are numerous individuals that need to begin profiting with recordings, however they are unequipped for making proficient quality recordings for themselves. You can assist these individuals with creating top notch recordings for their venture on an independent premise. Along these lines, you can acknowledge their requests to make, alter or even market recordings and get paid for the administrations that you give them. Obviously, you can likewise offer your video generation administration locally for extraordinary occasions, for example, weddings and business gatherings.

3. Make Video Lessons

In the event that you are a topic master in a specific specialty or point, it's a good thought for you to begin making preparing recordings identified with your specialty. Step by step instructions to and instructional exercise recordings, help your group of spectators adapt more data about a subject they are keen on, just as to take care of their issues. For example, on the off chance that you are a health specialist, you can make video exercises about how to do activities to get in shape, how to do activities to pick up muscle, how to do certain activities effectively, and so on.

You can offer your recordings by means of a membership administration, where your customers pay a month to month or yearly expense for proceeded with access to your recordings, you can offer them online on a compensation for each view premise or you can sell your recordings as a pack by means of download or by sending them on plate or other memory stockpiling gadget. You can conceivably profit with recordings beginning today by making and selling instructional exercise recordings.

4. Sell Your Stock Footage

Like stock photographs, there are likewise online administrations that sell stock film for business use. These stock recordings and "b-move" cuts are generally utilized by business video makers to finish their tasks. On the off chance that you can make proficient recordings of fascinating subjects, you can begin selling your stock film through those sites and profit with recordings immediately. Remember that on the off chance that you sell stock film through these sites you will part income of all offers of your recordings the specialist organization that has your stock film; they have the video, handle the exchanges and market their site. In the event that your recordings have a specific subject or center, as submerged video film, for instance, you can likewise sell stock film straightforwardly through your very own site. In the event that you have an enormous enough reach, you could conceivably begin making with your recordings rapidly, yet for most video business visionaries it will require a long time to manufacture a gainful market.

5. Subsidiary Advertising and Selling Product Placement on Viral Videos

Another approach to profit with recordings is to make or secure the rights to viral recordings and afterward sell item position or subsidiary items through those recordings. Viral recordings are short pieces that individuals will appreciate watching and sharing. You can make motivating, interesting, questionable or passionate recordings and offer them by means of your internet based life records trusting that your social associations will remark and share your recordings among their companions and that they will impart them to their companions, as well – however that is the most difficult way; there's no assurance a video will circulate around the web and you may make one hundred of them before viewing a video get on and spread quickly.

Hanging around or while going around the nation means going with friends to some party night. An incredible workstation that is stacked with altering programming, hard drive of film, and a respectable pair of earphones is extremely all you need. Having a work area with additional screens, full keyboard mouse, monster speakers, USB center points and all that are incredible, however unnecessary.

For what apparatus you do require,

10 years prior, not too bad quality video configurations were all the while being caught onto tape and other proprietary frameworks, requiring control decks and catch cards that were more costly than my truck. Nowadays I'm ready to alter for offices who value the all-computerized work process as much as I do. Without a doubt, they at times shoot on DSLRs, however I consistently get film shot on BMCCs, mid to top of the line Sony frameworks, Canon C-Series, and the sky is the limit from there. All media winds up on a hard drive which is simpler for them, and keeps it simple (and modest!) for me.

Have an inclination that binge spending? Alright, here's a rundown of things that I utilize day by day in my home office. It makes the experience more pleasant and bit increasingly proficient, so I've developed this after some time.

Macintosh Macbook Pro with maximized RAM and an OWC SSD Startup Disk

Sony MDR 7506 Headphones

USB Hub

DisplayPort to VGA Adapter (for outer screen 1)

Precious stone USB to VGA Adapter (for outer screen 2)

OWC Mercury Elite Pro Mini External Hard Drives

Logitech MediaPlay Wireless Mouse

In the event that you don't have a work process or customers nailed down, start by altering a couple of basic activities for individuals you have worked with before. Do an in the background alter, or volunteer to do a promotion or something to that affect for them. (Reward tip: Do it for somebody who has a huge online life following so it gets a ton of additional traffic, and potential referrals!) Editing a couple of spec activities will cause you to experience every one of the paces in question, and you'll begin to refine your work process while building your altering portfolio. Which leads me to the self evident…

Have a strong altering reel or instances of work, on the web and prepared to appear

When requesting for work, you'll have to give verification of aptitude. Either a few decent, short alters you've taken a shot at, or an assemblage reel of segments of various altering ventures. It has a couple of various completed video alters to flaunt, however try to send the alter that will be most similar to what your potential customer is needing you to accomplish for them.

Get your stockpiling within proper limits

After my initial couple of employments, I understood that I needed nearby stockpiling for my media and my reinforcements, however I needed to reinforcement customer drives too. That is to say, consider the possibility that when I dispatched the drive back the Fedex bundle was lost or harmed. I chose to become tied up with a capacity framework that addressed my issues, and I've been utilizing these drives for a considerable length of time. The OWC Elite Pro (minis) hard drives are little, can be transport controlled, tastefully coordinate my Apple items, and out of around 20-30 drives I've acquired for myself, customers, and companions, I've never had a solitary one turn sour. I can't suggest them enough.

Prepared to work? Contact your friends (once more) and take to the virtual worlds!

Quite a bit of my work has originated from other video makers or rehash customers, where I altered a venture once for them, conceivably at their area, and had the option to keep on working with them even subsequent to moving the nation over. It was as simple as telling them that I had the capacities to telecommute and that I could transfer alters for them. All they have to do is Fedex me a drive and I'll wrap up (pretty much!)

Makers I've worked for have alluded me to other people, so I've included a few customers from verbal exchange alone. Other than the previously mentioned, assets like Mandy.com, the Creative Cow Job Search, ProductionHub, and even here and there Craigslist have yeilded ventures. Facebook has turned into another way I've looked for some kind of employment also, by adding myself to gatherings identified with video or photography, and joining discussions when I saw a chance to network and offer my administrations.

Have a record sharing help prepared to utilize

Working remotely, I'll regularly get sent a hard drive with film. In the next week that I'm altering, unavoidably there will be some still photographs, illustrations, or different records I have to get from the maker. Great makers will more often than not have a record move administration set up, yet you may need to offer an answer too in the event that they don't. Google Drive or Box.com have functioned admirably for me previously. They are free and take care of business. In the event that you have your own FTP server for your site you can utilize that, and there are additionally administrations like Nimia.com that offer document moves and talk abilities, notwithstanding different highlights.

Work quick and quick

Makers have a lot of alternatives for video editors, and for them to work with somebody remotely you need to make it as simple as feasible for them, and give a speedy turnaround. This can mean working during that time to get an unpleasant slice to them the following morning. I'm 2 hours behind the east coast, so I'm either up late the principal night or up promptly the following morning to blast out a harsh cut before the accompanying work day is accomplished for my customers. I'd bet this is one reason I get rehash business.

Track your time.

On the off chance that charging continuously and not the task, I utilize a clock on my telephone as a kind of advanced punch clock. There are a few applications for both your work area and cell phone that can do this, so there's no explanation you can't follow your time. You will charge precisely, yet additionally get an extraordinary thought of to what extent it takes you to do alters, which will assist you with quoting employments better later on.

Use fares or renders to take breaks.

I do this constantly. I'll work until I hit a characteristic delay, either from rendering, sending out, or moving documents. While these run, I'll eat, take the canine out, or on account of sending out a long alter, I'll set it up to run medium-term. Thusly I'm not sitting around during business hours, when I could be accomplishing more work.

Mark, sort out, and make it sham verification.

In case you're a decent proofreader, odds are you do this as of now. On the hard drive your customer sends you, make an organizer named with your name and the task name. Inside it, subfolders isolating music, illustrations, venture records, and everything else, will help keep things perfect and sorted out for the person who opens this up on the customer end. I've been on phone calls with customers in the past in light of the fact that I didn't mark organizers appropriately and it made me look terrible when they couldn't locate a specific record. Exercise learned!

Use Vimeo for unpleasant cuts and even finished editions.

With a Vimeo Plus record, I'm ready to transfer recordings and secret phrase ensure them. I'll do this for harsh cuts on the activities I'm altering. Vimeo is a truly available spot to watch recordings from, and my customers can even download the document in the event that they have to.

Refreshing the video on vimeo with another alter form takes only a tick.

✱ Make Money from Creating Animations Videos

The interest to make money with videos online has never been higher. Bloggers, new digital market platform, known media organizations and brands are shouting out for quality short movies. The animated films that can be streamed, keeping in mind the end goal are to manufacture glory. To gain refinement and direct people to their online networking or social media.

Can we make money with videos online?

While wanting to make a short film, there must be somebody who knows you came and make this Inquiry about: How to make money online with animated video? You at that point say a confused response to. Now we ask you: For what valid reason? Without expecting a budgetary advantage, why you want to know? What's more, why you didn't use the accessible business possibilities for gaining cash from your animated videos.

We realize that there are too many blogs that are purposed to show you about the approaches to profit from YouTube, no Budget filmmaking tips as such. While we chose to compose something about this point, one thing that we write about is— Never compose something that is not understandable.

In view of your film talk dialect region, start a joint effort with well running YouTube or Vemo channel that has a high volume of endorsers and begins a business association with all of them. Think about the partnership along ahead in long term.

Offering privileges for your animation video, influencing it as a component. if the fortunes support financer (Film Producer) will probably enables you to coordinate that film. Otherwise, you will get patent rights for utilizing the topic of the short film.

Are you decided to Create Animation Videos for YouTube Platform? Well, that is a great option for filmmakers and video creators to generate income from their videos. At present, the YouTube is having 1 billion users' presence and 300 hours of videos, upload to YouTube on Every Hour.

Numerous individuals pick filmmaking as their career and setting their minds to making cash is a basic thing. Making cash through filmmaking or animated videos isn't a straight street. You have to ensure quality work to win cash and be perceived. Developing short film industry now offers a bigger number of choices than it did a couple of years back. One can settle on the following approaches on how to make money online with animated video:

♣ Make your own YouTube channel and viral your video. Yet, this by itself isn't sufficient. You require no less than 80 people into your channel before you begin earning. Sites like YouTube search in terms for the number of subscribers.

♣ You can utilize online stages like Short fondly – A stage for creative movie producers or animated filmmakers to

           advance your work and pick up the
           crowd. To gain all the attention from your
           target audience.

♣   Participate in film celebrations. This will
           give you acknowledgement in the film
           business. As animation filmmaking is also
           growing day by day you can draw the
           attention towards your animated video.

♣   Post your animated videos at settled (well
           established) channels which will enable
           you to get viewers and supporters in
           extensive numbers. All that subscription
           in large number through a known site.

Most likely the simplest and least expensive answer for the
less technically knowledgeable individuals, or for the
individuals who do not have a large audience. For $199/
year in addition to 10% of your profit, you'll have the
capacity to sell your animated videos directly on Vimeo.
Much the same as offering on Amazon, the huge preferred
standpoint. The large number of viewers, willing to pay to
watch quality movies. In the event that you don't have your
own audience, adding yourself to an extensive accessible
site (Searchable source) of movies may be a decent
method to discover your clients or your target audience.

On the off chance that you have your own site, and have
some sort of following. You can offer your animated
videos specifically to them. There are numerous tools for
offering advanced items, there are only a couple of them:

♣   Gum road

♣   Woo commerce

♣   Wistia

♣   Amazon S3

Nothing is impossible in this era, you can actually make money with videos online. Follow your passion for the animation and you can make money with videos online easily.

YouTube views:

This method is the simplest one, but probably the least effective. You make a short, upload it to YouTube, monetize your channel by enabling ads and watch the money flows.

Here's why it's not the most effective method, though: Let's say you make 2 animated shorts per year, which is INCREDIBLY hard to do. Then, let's say each short gets 5 Million views by some stroke of luck from the virality God. Your total revenue for that year will then be around $10,000. And again, that's with the unlikely scenario of managing to produce 2 very popular animated shorts in one year.

YouTube not a great platform for animators because it relies on watch time and frequency of uploads. These two factors create a lot of difficulty for animators, since it takes such a long time to create a short animation, and it's usually pretty short. That's one of the reasons gaming channels do so well, they upload almost every day and their videos can go on for a long long time.

However, there is a way an animation channel can do great on YouTube, and that's by creating content around your shorts. This is what I've done since the beginning.

Uploading making-of videos, tutorials and production-vlogs. If you only upload your shorts you will have a hard time getting traction, but if you create some momentum around it with other content, you will have an easier time growing on YouTube.

The more popular YouTube animators often resort to a limited animation style, more similar to an animatic, and almost always in 2D. That way they can produce much more videos. Here is the list of some of our favorite YouTube animation channels.

Selling your short

Selling your animated short directly to your audience can be much more profitable. Say you sell it for $5, you will only need 2000 views to get to that $10,000 figure we talked about earlier. But that also means you'll have to get 2000 people to buy your film, which isn't an easy task, especially if you haven't spent time building an audience.

When we launch our next short Tasteful it will be much easier for us to sell it (since we've been talking about it for such a long time and have been building a following for the past 3 years) compared to someone who simply releases their short out of thin air.

Here are some of the ways you can sell your short directly to your audience:

Vimeo on Demand

Probably the easiest and cheapest solution for the less tech-savvy people, or for those who does not have a large audience. For $199/year plus 10% of your earnings, you'll be able to sell your animated short directly on Vimeo. Just like selling on Amazon, the big advantage here is the exposure to a large pool of primed viewers, willing to pay to watch quality films. If you don't have your own audience, adding yourself to a large searchable source of films might be a good way to find your customers.

Amazon / iTunes

I don't have experience with selling on these platforms, but I know that many people use them. iTunes could get costly (sometimes paying thousands to aggregators for posting your film) and Amazon can be used for free. You'll have to do a bit more research on that if that's the path you think about taking.

Sell on you own site

This is something I have more experience with. If you have your own site, and have built some kind of following, you can sell your shorts directly to them. There are many tools for selling digital products, here are just a few I'm familiar with, either from personal use or from recommendations:

1. Easy Digital Downloads (A shopping cart plugin for WordPress)

1. Gumroad (A super easy-to-use tool for selling digital products)

1. Woocommerce (The most popular shopping cart plugin)

1. Wistia (A high-quality video hosting company, for hosting your animated short)

]   Amazon S3 (Amazon's cloud storage tool, for
letting your customers download your film
to their computers)

Merchandize

An indirect way to make money from your film, having
merchandize could work for you, especially if your film is
on the cuter side, making plush dolls or pillow cases a
viable thing to sell. Sites like Society6 let you upload
designs and then sell a large verity of products with
those designs. Anything from mugs to posters to hoodies.

For example: When we release Tasteful we will be selling
an art-of book with concept art, character designs etc. This
would be a great accompanying product for the film,
providing great value to the viewer as well as helping us
maintain a sustainable business

CHAPTER 2
EARN MONEY FROM SIMPLE JOB

★ **Earn Money From Simple Jobs**

•Virtual Assistant

With so many businesses operating mostly, or even completely, online, it's no wonder that many hire virtual assistants to help keep them organized and complete administrative tasks. According to the International Virtual Assistants Association, these workers are "independent contractors who (from a remote location, usually their home or office) support multiple clients in a variety of industries by providing administrative, creative, and technical services."

Although virtual assistant jobs vary drastically, tasks can include composing and responding to emails, creating and distributing business-related documents, responding to media and business inquiries, writing and creating content, and more. Check out virtual assistant jobs at sites such as Upwork.com and Zirtual.com.

While pay varies, virtual assistants can typically charge between $15 and $75 an hour. However, what you'll earn depends on who you work for and the level of skill required for your daily tasks.

Anybody can turn into a menial helper and get paid to do what they cherish. I've demonstrated it!

One of the main dollars I at any point earned as an online entrepreneur was by working for another business person as her Marketing Assistant.

I advanced her digital books through looking into and making posts for visitor blogging efforts, making points of arrival for online courses, composing follow up email groupings for pamphlets, and dealing with her web based life stages.

If I somehow managed to begin my online business once more I'd at present do it a similar way!

Working for a progressively experienced business person enabled me to become familiar with the ropes, see in the background of her business, and approach her cerebrum. She tutored me as well as it resembled I got paid to learn!

That is the best part about making cash as somebody's remote helper, overseeing editorial manager, or venture supervisor. You gain admittance to the internal functions of their business all while getting paid.

In case you're hoping to turn into a remote helper, and make cash helping different entrepreneurs, presently's ideal time to start.

Remember to snatch this free manual for 150+ administrations you can offer as a remote helper! Turning into a menial helper with no experience
At the point when I initially propelled this blog in 2011 I truly had no clue what I was doing. I mishandled around, composed a couple of blog entries, and posted a couple of tweets on Twitter. It wasn't until I ardently begun perusing

different online journals about business and enterprise that my vocation improved.

In the wake of pursuing a few bulletin records and "stalking" a couple of business people via web-based networking media, I handled the gig a couple of days after the fact! We worked out an installment bargain where I got paid $16 an hour for around 32 hours of work every month. The rate and work expanded after some time and I in the end moved to a month to month retainer plan that worked out to generally $25 60 minutes. I worked with this customer for 2.5 years and she gave me a sparkling tribute. In case you're figuring it out, $16 an hour X 32 hours every month = $512 in my first month!

That's right, inside my first month of being a remote helper I had the option to acquire over $500! Furthermore, this return in 2012 so envision the amount more cash you could win now.

Here are the means you can profit as an amateur menial helper in only 30 days.

1. Land your first customer

Finding your first customer is startling — you're putting yourself out there and feel like you have no cracking thought what you're doing.

Uncertainty begins to sneak in and you're asking why on the planet anybody would pay you for your ability and aptitudes.

This is the reason it's savvy to begin as a VA by utilizing a sidelong ability.

I don't get this' meaning? The fastest method to begin getting paid is to advertise an ability you definitely know. This can be founded on past involvement, a vocation confirmation, or past information.

Transform something you definitely realize how to do into the establishment for your VA business. In the event that you went to class for bookkeeping, start an accounting or advanced association business.

Influence your past experience to grandstand abilities that are as of now in your resume.

2. Offer VA administrations customers need

When you have a potential activity you need to apply for, you need an outline of administrations or bundles of your present contributions. There are truly unlimited assignments and administrations you can offer to different business visionaries: Email the board Web based life booking

Showcasing and online classes Blog the board Digital book advancement and visitor blogging, Independent composition Altering and copywriting Looking into and actuality checking The rundown goes on... Restricted down your concentration by just offering 1-3 bundles dependent on past experience and stir your way up from that point. Rundown the essential errands for each, start/ end dates, what each bundle + rate incorporates, any installment subtleties, a customer tribute, and a connect to your portfolio.

3. Make a site or portfolio

When you have your lord rundown of VA administrations you can utilize this to help make the bundles/contributions on a site or portfolio page.

On the off chance that you don't have a Services page or the like it's an ideal opportunity to set one up. This can be known as a "work with me" page, "enlist me" page, or whatever else.

You need to give potential customers a spot to see your contributions and check whether you're a solid match, just as making it idiotically simple for them to get in touch with you. The less taps the better!

Two instances of changing over Service pages:
Look at Kristin's Hire Me page. She took a shot at unmistakably characterizing her bundles, streamlining her page, and setting her rates. Also, as a result of this she as of late had her best pay month yet!

My Hire Me page is upgraded for the hunt term "remote helper" so when anybody types that expression into Google, my page is one of the primary outcomes.
An agenda for your Service page to turn into a menial helper:
What your identity is and what you offer (in addition to what you don't!)
Past experience, models, portfolio Present and past customers Contributions, administrations, bundles Points, industry, and so on Current rates (or beginning rates)
Tributes from current customers A contact structure

4. Charge continuously versus a level rate

In the first place phases of offering VA benefits it's ideal to charge customers constantly. It's hard to completely see how rapidly you work and to what extent certain ventures will take you.

Try not to place yourself in the situation of working for a considerable length of time and days and not getting appropriately made up for it.

When you realize to what extent the sorts of administrations you offer take you, and the aggregate sum of work they involve, you should change to a month to month expense or level rate as opposed to charging continuously.

For email the executives work you may definitely realize that it will take you 1-2 hours out of each day, 5 days per week, so you could offer this administration for a level $400 every week (which works out to be $40 60 minutes). Snap here to turn into a menial helper today!

Some VA work is simpler to pinpoint how a lot of work is included while others are increasingly conceptual and will take some experimentation.

The going rate for VA work begins at $20 every hour and can be as much as $50 every hour. You can acknowledge a much lower rate however more often than not this is possibly shrewd in case you're very unpracticed. After that it's imperative to build your costs and request raises consistently.

The more specific your VA contributions are, the more every hour you can charge. It likewise relies upon your customer and their industry of work.

A non-benefit customer won't have the option to manage the cost of about as much as a money related organization can. Try not to be hesitant to begin charging constantly and afterward change to a level rate.

This will enable you to have more opportunity with how you invest your energy, and cut back on your administrator hours when making solicitations toward the month's end.

5. Learn constantly

A significant piece of turning into a remote helper is that you're continually learning and improving your specialty. Online entrepreneurs and business visionaries frequently need assistance with tech-related issues and testing out new social stages or business devices.

What's more, YOU can be the one to assist them with this! Nonetheless, so as to do this adequately it's imperative to learn constantly. You ought to normally be putting resources into yourself, sharpening your aptitudes, and expanding your insight. This should be possible through tuning in to digital broadcasts, perusing business books, and putting resources into classes and courses.

Step by step instructions to turn into a remote helper

In case you're prepared to begin acquiring your first $500 this month, here are the means to take; Locate your optimal customer and tail them via web-based networking media Influence past involvement to arrive your first customer

Concoct an ace rundown of administrations to offer as a remote helper

Set up together an unmistakable Services page or portfolio Upgrade your Services page for the best outcomes Charge continuously then move to a level rate Keep expanding your rates and costs Furthermore, you can begin at the present time! Download the free manual for 150+ Virtual Assistant Services to Offer Clients. Making a move today will enable you to kick off your VA profession so you can begin accomplishing your fantasies about bringing home the bacon from home.

•Medical Transcriptionist

Although many medical transcriptionists work for hospitals or physician's offices, most are able to work at home, and at a time or place of their choosing. Since their tasks involve transcribing recorded medical dictation, a computer, desk, and earpiece are generally the only requirements after completing a postsecondary medical transcriptionist program.

According to the Bureau of Labor Statistics (BLS), medical transcriptionists earned a national median wage of $35,720 in May of 2016, or $17.17 an hour. Although many medical transcriptionists are self-employed, many find jobs through their local hospital, physician, or community college or vocational school.

•Translator

According to the Bureau of Labor Statistics, most translators do their work at home, and often under tight deadlines. Although some need a bachelor's degree, the most important requirement for translators is, of course, fluency in at least two languages.

As the BLS notes, around 22% of translators were self-employed in 2016. The majority were spread among these industries: professional, scientific, and technical services (30%); state, local, and private educational services (23%); hospitals (8%); and government (6%).

The national median wage for this career was $46,120 in 2016, although the top 10% of workers earned an average of $83,010. Look for job postings for translators on sites like Upwork.com.

Web Developer

•Travel Agent

Although the demand is expected to decrease over the next decade, the opportunities are still there for travel agents who can harness the Internet to earn clients and help them plan their adventures. According to the BLS, job prospects may be best for travel agents who offer expertise in certain regions of the world, have experience planning tours or adventures, or who focus on group travel.

Around 15% of travel agents were self-employed in 2016, but the vast majority of the rest of them worked in the travel arrangement and reservation services industry. Travel agents earned a national median wage of $36,460 in 2016.

★ Freelance Writer

More than ever, writers are needed to formulate news articles, create content, and come up with the creative ideas that fill the pages of nearly every site on the Internet. And although many bigger sites have in-house writers, a growing number of sites outsource their content and hire freelance writers and content creators. Writing experience is very helpful, but what you really need to get started are drive, ambition, and the ability to find a unique angle on events that happen every day.

Sites like Upwork.com list online freelancing positions, as does Freelancer.com and Media Bistro. To get hired, you'll likely need to have a portfolio of solid work, or at least some writing samples you can include with your resume. While writing fees vary depending on the job and the freelancer, many writers earn at least $150 per article and some earn up to $1,500 per finished piece. The BLS notes that writers earned a median wage of $61,240 nationally in 2016, although the top ten percent of workers earned around $118,640.

What You'll Need so as to Make Money Freelancing Online

Abilities People Want to Buy

A consultant is a person who performs administrations for a charge, regardless of whether that is hourly, per word, or per venture. At the end of the day, specialists exchange time for cash.

In this manner, you have to have abilities individuals are eager to pay for. You can get innovative here! Such huge numbers of individuals figure they don't have the experience to turn into a specialist, however I challenge you to survey your history.

Have you at any point had work? Assuming this is the case, that implies you DO have aptitudes individuals will pay you for! The most straightforward change from representative to specialist is to begin with the things you've just been paid to do.

For instance, before I turned into a consultant, I was chipping away at the advertising group of a startup. So when I chose to go independent, what did I do? I began selling advertising administrations (web-based social networking the board, copywriting, PR crusades, and so on.) to new companies! It was a basic progress since I could utilize the work I did as a worker as my portfolio as a consultant.

In the event that regardless you think you do not have the right stuff to turn into a specialist, there is a sort of outsourcing work you ought to thoroughly consider: being a remote helper.

I think about the menial helper as the passage level occupation in the independent world. Much like a secretary can proceed to turn into the workplace chief, a menial helper can proceed to turn into an online business administrator, an advertising expert, a website specialist, and extremely some other "more elevated level" independent position!

What's a remote helper? A remote helper helps an individual or business with practically any assistance possible. There are remote helpers for:

- travel booking
- appointment planning
- email the board
- graphic plan
- social media the board
- proofreading

For instance, suppose you need to be an expert independent supervisor, however you've just done a couple altering occupations and don't feel you're able to be a full-time independent editorial manager. You can begin as a menial helper who offers editing administrations. The thing that matters is that you'll get paid not exactly on the off chance that you were an independent manager, however in the end, you can elevate yourself to proofreader and charge a higher rate since you'll have assembled your portfolio as a menial helper.

Activity STEP: If you've thought hard everything you could, yet come up short on the abilities to turn into a specialist: adapt new aptitudes by means of online courses!

Some Ideas from top courses:

- Pinterest Traffic Avalanche – This will support you in the event that you'd like to deal with business' Pinterest records to enable them to direct people to their locales and, at last, make more income. I've taken this course and prescribe it!

•Making Sense of Affiliate Marketing – This will support you in the event that you'd like to turn into a partner director helping bloggers and different organizations increment their subsidiary income. I've taken this course as well. Look at my audit of it.

•Earn More Writing – This will support you on the off chance that you'd like to turn into an independent essayist. The course was made by a functioning independent essayist who makes six figures from her composition work.

•30 Days or Less to Freelance Writing Success – Another independent composition course that will tell you the best way to transform your composition abilities into a business quick.

•30 Days or Less to Virtual Assistant Success – An incredible method to break into outsourcing is through turning into a remote helper. VAs are required by bloggers, specialists, independent companies and even enormous organizations. You can do anything from regulatory to plan to composing work.

A Reliable Internet Connection

In case you will work remotely as a specialist, you will require a solid Internet association. For my kindred Americans and others in the First World, this is normally not an issue. It turns into an issue, in any case, on the off chance that you choose to travel while working.

At whatever point I travel to progressively remote regions, I have a few alternatives helpful to get to Internet out and about:

- T-Mobile
- Verizon JetPack

On the other hand, you can simply adhere to computerized wanderer well disposed spots. On the off chance that you need to go off-the-framework, ensure you complete your work early and take an appropriate get-away —free of any independent work.

A Personal Computer / Laptop

You could utilize a personal computer, yet in the event that you'll be in a hurry a ton, a workstation is a superior choice. I utilize this PC, and it's been ideal for my run of the mill assignments, which include:

- Typing in Google Docs
- Editing pictures in Photoshop
- Light video altering with Camtasia
- Sending messages
- Transcribing sound
- Uploading pictures to WordPress

A Domain / Website

As an online specialist, you need a site. This is your "online customer facing facade," and in addition to the fact that it serves as your portfolio, it additionally demonstrates you're genuine.

In spite of mainstream thinking, it doesn't cost a great deal of cash and you don't must have coding abilities to dispatch a site. Indeed, you can even form your independent site for FREE.

Instructions to Make Money Freelancing Online in 7 Steps

Stage 1: Decide what you will sell.

Sounds basic enough, isn't that so? As I discussed above, you'll have to assess what aptitudes you have and how you can transform those into administrations individuals will need to purchase.

Stage 2: Decide who you need to work with (your optimal customers).

Know your circle and work with the best candidates, hire experienced Person with the right expertise for your work.

Stage 3: Price and bundle your administrations.

Making sense of how to value your administrations as a consultant will be one of the most difficult and essential things you do while setting up your independent business. I obsessed about my rates for a considerable length of time when I began. I likewise seriously undervalued my administrations in the first place, to such an extent that I was working continually yet always broke.

(Individual costs + operational expense + reserve funds)/. 7 = Revenue Goal

The .7 speaks to 70%, as in, 30% goes to expenses, and you keep 70% to use for yourself. Presently, annual duties are entangled and fluctuate generally. Most specialists inform putting aside 25% with respect to your independent pay to settle regulatory expenses. On the off chance that you make more than the normal specialist, 30% might be better (it additionally relies upon where you live). Be that as it may, I've discovered that 30% is all that anyone could need. On the off chance that you spare TOO a lot, it's route superior to sparing close to nothing!

Since the title of this post is the means by which to make your $5,000/month as a consultant, we'll use $5,000 every month for instance target objective. In the event that you make $5,000 in REVENUE, that implies that after 30% of assessments is taken out, you get the opportunity to keep $3,500 in PROFIT.

Along these lines, for this model, ensure your own costs, operational expense, and whatever sum you put in a safe spot for reserve funds doesn't surpass $3,500. On the off chance that it does, at that point your objective income very to be higher than $5K.

Stage 4: Create your site.

You NEED a portfolio site to prevail upon customers as a consultant. Be that as it may, it doesn't need to cost a lot of cash. You can even make a portfolio site for nothing. In case you're an independent essayist, you can utilize Contently to make a free portfolio site that exhibits your connections.

Stage 5: Find perfect potential customers (prospecting)

Presently, you have to go out and make a rundown of potential customers alongside their contact data (email address and first name is fine).

In case you're trapped, here are 11 spots online to discover independent gigs:

- AngelList
- Working Nomads

- Flexjobs
- RemoteOK.io
- Facebook gatherings
- Craigslist
- Cold messaging your preferred brands
- Friends and family
- Your expert system or different specialists
- Your boss or past businesses

Stage 6: Pitch them (outbound promoting)

While I'm a fanatic of inbound advertising, when you're simply beginning, you don't have the opportunity to squander. You should pitch potential customers forcefully.

State 7: Conduct disclosure calls

When you've pitched some potential customers, you ought to hear over from a few. Now, it's a great opportunity to book a revelation call or beginning interview. This is fundamentally where you jump on the telephone (or video talk) with a prospect and attempt to choose in case you're a solid match for one another.

Presently, don't get frightened, however this is a business call. In addition to the fact that you want to choose in case you're a solid match, yet you additionally need to let the big dog eat on the off chance that you conclude that you are.

Numerous new specialists have revelation call tension. Everything I can say is that I did as well, and it improves time and practice. The more revelation calls you do, the more calm you will feel.

Stage 8: Negotiate

No entrepreneur is insusceptible to exchange. It's the name of the game, and as a consultant, you should generally expect it.

Here are a couple of potential situations and how you can respond:

•If the customer needs to consult on cost: Except for unique cases, I'm a firm devotee that you ought to NEVER consult on cost, just on SCOPE. That implies if your charge for a 5-page site is $3,000, yet the customer demands they can just bear the cost of $2K, at that point possibly you chop it down to a 3-page site.

•If the customer needs to consult on extension: Be available to this current; it's thoroughly fine! Simply make sure to alter your charges as needs be.

•If the customer needs to consult on course of events: You reserve each privilege to charge a surge expense if a customer needs something done rapidly.

•If the customer isn't sure they need to work with you: Tread cautiously. Vulnerability some of the time can be a warning for an issue customer—one who continually changes scope on you and makes you overhaul and reconsider in light of the fact that they're not in any case sure what they need. Nonetheless, once in a while, they're amazing customers—they simply need all the more persuading that YOU are the correct specialist for them. In those cases, I offer a shorter paid time for testing. Thump it out of the recreation center during the paid preliminary, and they'll be anxious to keep on working with you. You can likewise offer a free preliminary or an unconditional promise.

•If the customer needs to attach additional administrations outside of what you ordinarily offer: Tread cautiously. If its all the same to those additional administrations are something you offering, I state let it all out, yet make certain to attach additional charges for it! On the off chance that those additional administrations are something you would prefer not to offer, at that point hold fast.

•Social Media Manager

Almost every big business has gotten on the social media bandwagon as a means to reach their customers directly, and without paying heavily for television, print, or radio ads. But not every big business has someone to manage their social media accounts, which is why more individuals have begun marketing themselves as social media managers and helping businesses grow their online following and expand their reach.

Although very little data are available for this work-at-home job since it is relatively new, thousands of listings for social media managers can be found on sites like CareerBuilder.com, SimplyHired.com, and Upwork.com. If you have a demonstrated command of social media and a sizable following, you might even be able to get started by reaching out to companies directly and asking if they need help.

Social media managers typically earn the same as a virtual assistant, with hourly rates of $15 – $75 fairly common. Some social media managers also work for a retainer or monthly fee, however.

★Data Entry Jobs

wide range of businesses need workers to enter various data into their systems, whether that data are used to track inventory or shipments, create business plans, or measure performance or output. And since a computer and typing skills are the most important requirements for this job, many data entry workers are able to work at home, and on a schedule that fits their lives.

According to the BLS, data entry workers earned a national median wage of $30,100 in 2016, although the top 10% earned more like $45,360. Since many data entry jobs are at-home jobs, you can always find dozens of data entry job postings on sites like Upwork.com, Freelancer.com, and SimplyHired.com, as well as dozens of others.

1. Captcha Entry Job

Captcha entry is becoming one of the hottest online data entry job. Although income is less than other job but its very simple & available for everyone.

You will be given a software where you have to login with your username & password & then type the Captcha images. You can earn up to $500 per month from this job.

2. Copy & Paste

Here you have to copy text material from a word or excel file and paste into another word or excel file. It is very easy however, you need to be very careful. Good knowledge of English is very important because you have to read and understand things.

3. Micro Jobs

There are number of sites where you can join as a micro worker & work on different types of data task. One of the most recommended online data entry job for extra income.

There are dozens of sites that provide micro jobs where you can join & earn minimum $200+ a month working on simple tasks.

4. Survey Forms

Filling up survey forms is also a type of data entry work. Here you have to fill online forms provided by different survey sites.

Through this form, you give your feedback for a particular product which helps companies to design the best products for consumers.

5. Basic Typing Job

The first and basic data entry job is typing. Here you have to type anything into an excel spreadsheet or a word document.

You don't require any special skill other than typing speed of 30+ words per minute. If your speed is less than this & you want to do this then you have to improve the speed to reach 30+ WPM level.

6. Form Filling

Form filling data entry jobs are not very common but you can find them on Internet. Here you have to fill simple forms with given information. Sometimes information is not given and you have to find on your own.

7. Image to Text

Next is converting image to text. Here you have an image file containing text material and you need to write it down on a word document. To put it simple, you have to see from image file and write it down on a word document.

8. Medical Transcription

Medical Transcription is the most popular work from home job. Here you have to be on a phone and write things down what you listen. So it is bit different than regular data entry job. You need great listening skills and write it down as you listen.

9. Formatting

You have to format a word document. Formatting is not that easy as it is seen. You have to have full knowledge of work documents, things like indentation, aligning etc.So learn MS word.

10. Content Writing

Content writing is bit different than regular data entry job. Here you have to write articles and give it back to publishers. Here you need more of a writing skill than typing skills.

11. Catalog Data Entry Operator

Catalog data entry operator is about creating an inventory list in an excel spreadsheet. An inventory has many products and you have to write it down their serial number, product name, numbers in stock, price etc into an excel spreadsheet.

This is like a normal data entry job.

12. Proofreading and Copywriting

Like content writing proofreading and copywriting is also a data entry work. However, they are bit different than regular data entry jobs.

Here you have to good at English and typing speed is not required. You must be able to read articles and find out mistakes.

13. Medical Coding

Medical coding is data entry work where you have to write codes of various products. These products are medicine of different kinds.

You have to be careful while entering those medical codes. You need some experience to take this job.

14. Payroll Data Entry Operator

Payroll data entry operator is for creating a payroll list for various companies. You have to create a list of employee name, address, salary etc in Excel spreadsheet.

The job is very similar to the catalog data entry operator where you fill information about products in the inventory.

15. Email Processing

Email processing jobs are about processing emails. You have to read emails and find out what their content is about. You might be asked to process thousands of email in a day. The job could be very exciting.

Extra:- Customized Data Entry Jobs

This is not actually a specific kind of data entry jobs. Here you could be asked to do anything what a company has to say.

The job is not specified and customized according to the needs of the company. You job could be anything.

So these were some of the data entry jobs available on the Internet and offline. You need to find out more about these online jobs and prepare yourself to become a data entry operator.

★ Call-Center Representative

Many businesses need workers who can answer the phone at all hours, assist customers, and process orders or deal with returns. But since more businesses are operating online, a growing number of these jobs are going to customer service workers who work at home.

Being an at-home call-center rep requires a computer and may require specific software or equipment. A great phone voice helps as well, as does any experience in customer service, data entry, retail sales, or management. Dozens of sites list job openings for call-center representatives, including Upwork.com, Freelancer.com, and SimplyHired.com. However, you may also find listings offered by local businesses in your local newspaper. While it's hard to find exact pay for call center representatives who work at home, Glassdoor.com says this workers typically earn a base pay of around $30,000 per year.

How does a job where you can work from home and get paid to talk on the phone sounds to you?

If you're used to telephone work, then an at home customer service agent job could be an excellent way to make money.

The company is called VOIQ, and the job is making calls on behalf of major companies to people who have already expressed an interest in hearing from them – no cold calls.

You can set your own hours with no minimum requirement, and like any other legitimate work at home job, it doesn't cost you anything to get started.

What You Need to Know?

As a VOIQ agent, you take on the role of a professional call agent, but don't have the hassle of going to work in a call center. In fact, you can do your job from anywhere as long as you have certain things:

) you must have a smartphone, and it can be iPhone or Android

) you need a good Internet connection

) you must be over 21

) you should be experienced at working in a call center

You will also need to have a relatively quiet space in which to work uninterrupted during the hours you choose. It's important that you are professional in taking on this task, as you will represent the employing company to the public.

Of course, there may be time restrictions on when you can call the customers. Typically you would need to do your work between 8 AM and 6 PM, though it may depend on what time zones you and the customers are in.

For its part, VOIQ is the company employing you, which provides the necessary app and software for you to work, and gets the jobs from the various employing companies.

VOIQ typically asks its applicants for 2 to 5 years prior experience in a call center.

How You Can Apply

You apply online at voiq.com, filling out your personal details and answering some yes or no questions, such as "Do you have a quiet place to work from?" and "Do you have an Android device, iPhone or iPad?".

You then have to record some 60-second videos using the camera in your computer and answering relevant questions related to your previous and intended work.

It seems like there is no way to skip this step, so if you don't have a camera on your computer, you will need to borrow a friend's.

You're also required to submit your resume in order for them to review your application. In the TOS, they make it clear that they don't even review you until they have a resume in hand.

After that, it can take up to three days to hear back.

Whether they decide to employ you will obviously depend on your performance and speaking voice, as well as having the right answers to the mainly obvious questions.

What You Have To Do

You work with the mobile app which you can download from the iTunes App Store or the Google Play Store.

VOIQ will email you every time a new campaign starts, and you can go from there.

The app will give you a short tutorial guide for the particular campaign, telling you what to say, ask, or do. You need to become sufficiently familiar with this that it will sound natural when you talk to the customer.

After each call, you have to mark the call outcome.

This can be

) Busy

) Number no longer in service

) No one answered the phone

) Message delivered to voicemail

) Contact can't be reached at this number

) Contact requested to not be called again

) Contact asked to be called later

With some campaigns, you don't leave a voicemail, but mark the call as "asked to be called later" so that the contact is made at a later date.

How Much Do You Get Paid?

For your work, you will be paid $12 per hour, provided you work consistently.

This is equivalent to about $.30 per minute (for every phone call,) allowing time between calls.

You can get paid any time you've earned at least one dollar in your account.

VOIQ does not send out money on any regular schedule, you have to ask for it. The money arrives by PayPal a few days later.

Be aware that your recorded calls may be listened to by the Quality Assurance team before they approve and pay you. If you have worked in a call center, you will be familiar with the idea of supervisors listening in on your calls at random to make sure you're doing a good job – this is a similar idea for the remote application. VOIQ has to be sure that it maintains standards, in order to satisfy its clients.

Is It for You?

If you have some experience working in a call center, this may be the ideal opportunity. No longer do you have to fight through traffic to sit in one of many cubicles, but you can work this job from home or any other quiet place.

You have to be diligent and able to work without a set schedule, and have a pleasant professional approach to the task. Your work will be reviewed, and the best call agents will tend to have new work offered to them first, so it's worth making an effort.

In return, the rewards are decent and you get all the freedom that you want, doing a job that you are good at.

If you meet the qualifications, visit VOIQ and apply for their at home customer service agent position and start getting paid. Even if you do it part time, it still is a great way to earn some side income

★Blogger

Becoming a blogger is unlike any other work-at-home job in that you have to show up and build it yourself. Even worse, the vast majority of blogs make zero dollars for years as they grow and become established. In that sense, blogging isn't much of a job at all.

However, there is a lot of potential for writers who are able to build an audience, grow their site, and find a way to monetize it and start earning an income. Some of the ways bloggers make money include affiliate advertising, sponsored posts, Google Adsense, and product sales. Even better, owning a blog can be an inexpensive way to start your own business, with domains costing an average of $12 per year and Web hosting costing as little as $7.99 per month.

. Start a blog and make money

1. Building Your Readership

There are bunches of approaches to adapt your blog once you have a decent number of guests. In any case, when you are simply beginning you won't have numerous perusers, so it's imperative to benefit as much as possible from every one. That implies that you have to ensure first-time perusers of your blog will return. Just by having returning perusers will you ever fabricate a sizable group of spectators that you can benefit from.

So how might you keep in contact with your perusers?

The most effortless and most ideal route is to approach them for an email address where you can reach them with updates. By gathering your perusers' email addresses from the earliest starting point of your blog you will manufacture the greatest mailing list conceivable.

Ever wonder why pretty much every site you go to requests you to join with your email address?

In showcasing there is an adage that "the cash is in the mailing list". This is on the grounds that a mailing rundown enables you to contact individuals again and again.

Each time you send an email to your rundown you can offer them items/administrations or simply get them to your visit your blog again where you can profit from advertisements (talked about beneath). This is actually what enormous organizations like Groupon do with their mailing records. They convey offers on a day by day or week by week premise

You will require an email showcasing administration to begin. By a wide margin the least demanding and most dependable that I have found is Constant Contact, which offers a free preliminary of their administrations for new bloggers. I have assembled a total bit by bit instructional exercise on the most proficient method to utilize Constant Contact with your blog.

2. Adapting Your Blog

When you have manufactured a nice readership base you can direct your concentration toward profiting from your blog. There an assortment of approach to do this, however one of the most worthwhile ways additionally happens to be the least demanding publicizing.

Having an enormous number of guests to your blog implies that publicists will pay to have their advertisements appeared to your perusers. The most effortless approach to blog for cash is to get paid for indicating commercials on your blog by joining Google's AdSense program at http://www.google.com/adsense

When you arrangement your record on AdSense you will be given a code to add to your blog. This code will naturally show notices on your blog from organizations who are a piece of Google's publicizing system. You may see promotions from little organizations identified with your theme, or you may see advertisements from enormous organizations that are totally inconsequential to your point.

The decent thing about AdSense is that you have a large number of promoters offering to publicize on your blog, and you should simply add the basic code to your blog. When you do that the procedure is totally distant.

Each time one of your guests taps on an advertisement, you get paid. Google gathers the cash from the promoters and after that writes you a check (typically consistently).

This game plan is decent in light of the fact that it is hands-off, but since you are managing a legitimate organization that you realize will really pay you on schedule.

What amount would you be able to make?

The sum that you can make from AdSense relies upon three variables:

1. The quantity of guests to your blog

This one is really self-evident. More individuals visiting your blog implies more taps on promotions, which means more cash for you.

2. The perceivability of the advertisements

At the point when you put the AdSense code on your blog you have a decision of the style of notices (huge pictures, little pictures, content, and so forth.) and furthermore where they are put. The more unmistakably the promotions are shown the almost certain they are to be clicked.

Notwithstanding, you need to adjust setting the promotions noticeably with the possibility of conceivably irritating your peruses. We have all visited sites where it's hard to see the substance because of the number and size of the advertisements. This is a sensitive equalization to accomplish and it's something you should try different things with to benefit from your blog.

3. The theme you are blogging about

The last factor that influences your AdSense pay is the point you are blogging about. This is on the grounds that publicists will pay more to be on sure web journals than they will for other people.

For instance, if your site is about golf, your perusers are probably going to have a sound pay. Along these lines, there are a decent number of publicists that need to get their promotions before your perusers, and they are probably going to pay a decent sum for every snap to do this.

Balance this with a blog about Justin Bieber. The perusers of this blog are probably going to be young ladies, who more often than not have relatively little buying force. In view of this promoters will probably save money on each snap.

These three elements will decide the measure of cash you make. Evaluating precisely what you will make is entirely troublesome, yet a high traffic blog on the correct subject can possibly get a few thousand dollars consistently. Obviously, numerous individuals procure not as much as this, and some acquire significantly more. Truth be told, it has been assessed that some top AdSense distributers gain about $2 million every year just from AdSense.

Remember that creation cash from your blog requires some serious energy. All things considered, there is an explanation that figuring out how to profit from a blog is the last advance in my guide. You have to ensure you have pursued all the past advances splendidly so as to give yourself the most obvious opportunity with regards to acquiring a considerable salary from blogging. This won't occur without any forethought, yet most bloggers find that the work itself is compensating enough to proceed on the adventure.

When you have your blog ready for action, make a point to look at my bit by bit instructional exercise on the most proficient method to introduce AdSense on your blog.

As a new blogger, it can be hard to know where to start. You hear people are making money from their blogs, but you don't quite understand how.

In this beginner's guide on how to make money with a blog for beginners, we're going to show you how to make your first $100 from your blog.

I know. $100 doesn't sound like a lot of money. But it's just the beginning. Once you get the basics down and earn your first income, you can scale it and earn as much money as you'd like.

Here is Even more with Make Money as a Blogger

First of all, it's significant for me to advise you that blog salary doesn't occur incidentally. You should set up a blog, fabricate a group of people who trusts you and drive traffic routinely before you can begin making a salary. The intriguing blogger's way of life that you see via web-based networking media accompanies a ton of diligent work so prepare sure you're to placed the work in. As a blogger learner, you most likely don't have huge amounts of traffic yet and don't have a colossal email list either. So the thought here is to begin little ($100) and develop from that point as your blog develops in size.

By defining yourself a reasonable objective of $100, you will feel roused – as a bigger objective may appear to be excessively out of sight reach. Also, when you do accomplish your objective, you will improve comprehension of what works for your blog (and what doesn't) and utilize the learnings to get significantly more cash-flow.

The most effective method to Start a Blog in Under 10 Minutes

•Blog Niches That Make Money: 5 Profitable Blog Niche Ideas (Examples Included)

•What Should I Blog About? 80+ Ideas You Can Create a Blog About

•How To Come Up With a Blog Name. 8 Creative Ideas To Pick The Perfect Name

This post may contain member joins. In the event that you click on them and buy something we get a little level of the deal. More information here

Blogging For Money – For Beginners So in any case, how DO you make cash blogging as a tenderfoot? Indeed, there are really various ways you could approach this. Give me a chance to separate them for you.

1. Offshoot Income

One of the least demanding and most basic approaches to make cash blogging, for fledglings, is member advertising. You don't have to have your very own items or administrations. You essentially advance other individuals' items on your blog, and when somebody makes a buy, you make a commission off it.

Where to Find Affiliate Programs

So where do you discover these associate projects? To be straightforward there are many choices and it might overpower when you're beginning.

Numerous new bloggers start by profiting with Amazon. So you sign up to turn into an Amazon Affiliate and use connects inside your blog. At the point when somebody makes a buy on Amazon, you will make a little commission of it.

Furthermore, you can join to utilize enormous member advertising systems. These systems have a great many offshoot programs for an assortment of brands. You can pick the brands and items you need to advance and do it from one brought together stage.

Two partner promoting systems we use ourselves:

1. ShareASale
2. Commission Junction

1. Make a rundown of items and administrations you adore and use. Research potential affiilate advertising open doors for these.

2. Sign up to Amazon and additionally partner advertising systems.

3. Conceptualize and make content that will enable you to advance your picked items and administrations.

For instance, in case you're advancing a product you like you use, you could make an instructional exercise on the most proficient method to utilize the product (for amateurs). Inside this article, you would utilize your member interface for the product so in the event that somebody navigates and makes a buy, you make the commission.

You could likewise do item audits as a bit of substance. This is a technique many style and magnificence blogger use. They will compose a survey of items they like to utilize and after that incorporate an associate connection so their perusers can make a buy.

There are numerous inventive and successful approaches to make content that brings subsidiary showcasing results. Do your examination and perceive how different bloggers in your specialty are advancing their subsidiary organizations.

Try not to be hesitant to acquire thoughts and imitate effective bloggers. You don't have to rehash an already solved problem.

4. Advance your substance. For you to profit from offshoot openings, your blog should be perused. Advance your substance via web-based networking media, by means of your email list and anyplace else that is important. The

more traffic you manufacture, the more the open doors for you to make partner salary.

2. Digital books

In the event that you need to sell your own items, a digital book is an incredible method to make cash blogging. It's additionally an incredible method to see whether your crowd is prepared to purchase from you.

Try not to get overpowered! A digital book is certainly not a novel. You don't need to compose several pages. Truth be told, most great digital books are succinct yet stuffed with data.

Think about a digital book as a more drawn out structure blog entry. You can make a digital book about practically any subject however clearly it would bode well to make it about a theme that is important to your perusers.

You should simply ensure it's a subject you know well and can expound on. What's more, obviously, it's a theme that is fascinating enough for your perusers to purchase from you.

Most apprentice bloggers will sell their first digital books at an entirely sensible cost. In this way, it's a smart thought to costs yours at $7 to $40 mark. That way, it is anything but a gigantic speculation for anybody to buy and you can sell it effectively.

Furthermore, for you… when you make a couple digital book deals, it's a colossal certainty sponsor. You know you're destined for success. You have individuals who need to purchase from you – you are currently prepared to take it to the following level.

When you've sold some digital books, you can take it further by making other advanced items, for example, online courses, video instructional exercises and furthermore online courses (which we talk about straightaway)

1. Conceptualize content thoughts: Analyze what substance reverberates with your group of spectators. What do they like finding out about? What subjects do you have skill in? What point connects with your group of spectators the most?

Ask yourself these inquiries to pick a digital book point that will

2. Compose the digital book: Keep things basic. You needn't bother with any extravagant programming. Start composing and organizing your digital book in Google Docs. You can structure an alluring spread utilizing Canva and you're all set.

3. Make sense of where to sell: To sell your digital book, you can utilize a wide range of stages:

1. All alone blog: Promote it wherever on your blog. Set up pennants in the sidebar, notice it in your blog entries and on the off chance that you have an email list – certainly let them realize you have a digital book available to be purchased.

2. On Amazon: You would self be able to distribute your book and sell it on Amazon effectively.

3. On ClickBank: ClickBank is an exceptionally famous online retailer for computerized items so selling your digital book on this stage can enable you to contact a wide group of spectators.

4. Set up for deals: Figure out how you will acknowledge installments and convey the digital book to your clients. You can do this effectively through a help like SendOwl (in case you're selling through your blog). Or on the other hand you can sell through Amazon or ClickBank as referenced previously.

You can likewise do your own arrangement, and acknowledge installments through a help like Paypal or Stripe and convey the digital books by means of email once you get an installment.

Do what is the most straightforward for you.

5. Advance your digital book: You have to get the word out about your digital book. Elevate your digital book to your email list, on Pinterest, on applicable Facebook gatherings and anyplace else that would be important. Try not to be modest to tell individuals you have something available to be purchased.

3. Online Courses

The subsequent stage up from digital books is making and selling on the web courses. Indeed, regularly bloggers will make a digital book and after that develop a similar theme in their online course.

Like digital books, you can make an online course about practically any point. Obviously, it ought to be a subject that individuals need to find out about and one you know a great deal about. At any rate enough to show a course.

A few thoughts... on the off chance that you have a nourishment blog, you can do a seminar on plans. On the off chance that you run a design blog, you could sell a seminar on style tips. In the event that you expound on connections, you could sell a seminar on the best way to oversee long separation connections.

You can sell your courses at more significant expense point than digital books yet the value you pick will truly rely upon the profundity of your course, your skill and how well your crowd definitely knows you.

I've seen short courses for $29, some for $47 and have likewise observed significant level specialists sell for $997. Research different courses in your specialty to perceive what the normal value point is.

Try not to overrate it yet don't undersell yourself either. Test a couple of costs and see what works best for you.

1. Pick a theme: Your course ought to be about a subject you can assist your group of spectators with. On the off chance that there's a battle or an issue that surfaces consistently, address it by making a course about.

2. Make your substance: Once your theme's set up, do the diligent work of arranging and making your course. There are numerous configurations to convey a course in yet most are normally a combo of recordings, slideshows and content.

Choose how you will convey data and make content in like manner.

You needn't bother with any extravagant hardware to begin. You can compose your contents in Google Docs and record your vides on your telephone (however utilize a tripod). Simply pick a peaceful spot and start making.

3. Make sense of where to sell: There are numerous approaches to sell a course on the web. A portion of your choices are:

⌐ All alone webpage: You can have your seminar all alone site

⌐ On Udemy (or other comparable destinations)

⌐ On Teachable (or other comparable stages.

⌐ Where you sell your course will likewise rely upon its intricacy. Stages like Teachable make it simple to make a course substantial on recordings and slideshows.

4. Set available to be purchased: Once individuals purchase your course, you will require an approach to convey the course to them.

At the extremely fundamental level, you can have your recordings on YouTube or Vimeo and convey it to your clients all alone site. To keep things basic, course makers regularly use stages, for example, Teachable or ClickFunnels. These stages help you have the course, yet additionally effectively acknowledge installments for your courses.
On the off chance that you've chosen to sell on Udemy to begin with, at that point the stage will manage you through the way toward setting up and selling a course through them.

5. Advance your course: Like everything else, in the event that you don't advance, nobody is going to know you

CHAPTER 3
ONLINE TRADING
FOREX/CRYPTO

How to make Money from Trading Online ?

In this section we will talk about Trading online by investing some money and then earn profit from it.

★Forex Trading

The foreign trade market is the world's most fluid market, with more than 5-trillion daily trading hands. The market is fluid 24-hours per day, 5-days every week, opening at night on Sunday during North American exchanging hours and shutting down at 5-pm on Friday evening during a similar time zone. On the off chance that you are an apprentice and simply dunking your toe into exchanging the forex markets, you ought to consider following the market and expanding your comprehension of why trade rates move before taking a chance with your well-deserved capital.

Find out About the Financial Markets

The monetary markets permit speculators, organizations, governments and national banks a spot to execute in an open market, trading their dangers to meet their money related needs. A corporate treasurer may need to trade benefits in Euros into dollars, similarly as a theorist accepts that the EUR/USD will rise. There are a great many reasons why trade rates and costs moved over a brief timeframe, creating commotion as members search at an ideal cost to enter or leave a position.

Before you start exchanging, you ought to find out about the various sorts of business sectors accessible to exchange, and which one you are most keen on following. Notwithstanding exchanging forex, you can likewise think about exchanging products, lists, and offers. The most ideal approach to find out about a market is to find out concerning why others trust it's moving and the various impetuses that may drive the cost or swapping scale a particular way. For instance, you may begin with searching for a style of investigation that is commonly given by trustworthy specialists, for example, Alpari. You will likely observe what kind of examination they offer and what sort of significant thoughts originate from the investigation they give. You can likewise glance through a specialist's instruction area and check whether they give data regarding why the business sectors move. Notwithstanding taking a gander at a dealer's training segment, you can check the business sectors for sites that attention on monetary markets instruction.

Figure out how to Do Your Own Analysis

There are two primary kinds of examination that forex brokers for the most part center around, which incorporate principal and specialized investigation. Crucial examination is the investigation of large scale occasions that will modify the course of a money pair. Specialized investigation is the investigation of value activity, including seeing force, patterns and inversion designs.

Principal Analysis

The essentials encompassing the forex markets depends on the financing costs markets of every one of the monetary forms that make up a conversion scale. For instance, in the event that you plan on exchanging the EUR/USD you need to have a measure of where loan costs are likely going in the Eurozone just as the United States. All in all, the more grounded an economy, the more probable the national bank is to raise loan fees, which help drive up market financing costs. The invert is likewise the situation for a more fragile economy where the national bank and market powers will probably drive loan fees lower.

The most ideal approach to decide whether an economy is solid is to have the option to assess nations budgetary data. This could incorporate their work data, their GDP, just as expansion data, for example, the shopper value record. Most trustworthy specialists will furnish you with a forex monetary schedule where you can perceive what market analysts anticipate that relative should history just as the real discharge. What is significant about basics is that each new snippet of data can change the heading of a swapping scale. On the off chance that the financial information is more noteworthy than or more terrible than anticipated, a swapping scale will move to mirror the new data.

Specialized Analysis

Specialized examination is the investigation of recorded costs. In spite of the fact that the past isn't constantly an indicator of things to come, various changes following explicit examinations can give you a check of where costs may move in the prospects. A portion of the more prominent specialized investigation studies incorporate assessing force. Force is the quickening or deceleration of value changes. In the event that you are keen on finding out about specialized investigation, you can take a gander at your merchant's instruction area, or pursue their specialized examination figures. There are additionally a few sites that will furnish you with training on various kinds of specialized investigation apparatuses. A portion of the more mainstream incorporate the MACD, the RSI, and Stochastics.

Discover great Broker

Your forex specialist encourages the execution of exchanges. While this is their most significant capacity, there are numerous highlights a representative like Alpari brings to the table which you ought to know about preceding storing assets at that merchant. In the first place, do some due industriousness. Look into audits by your forthcoming merchant and ensure there are no warnings. Misrepresentation cautions or issues with pulling back assets are the most significant. You likewise need to ensure there is proficient client care. You would prefer not to baffle yourself by finding an intermediary who won't respond to questions.

The following stage is to assess the stage. Does the dealer have training area or create specialized investigation conjectures? Furthermore, you need to ensure that your agent offers customers a money related schedule. Furthermore, you need to get some answers concerning the influence they give to customers. More elevated levels of edge will give you the choice to produce more income.

Start with a Demo Account

Most legitimate representatives will offer you genuine cash accounts just as showing accounts. A demo record is one where you are exchanging paper cash, not genuine capital. Most great exhibition records offer almost every one of the items that are accessible to exchange will a genuine cash account. The costs will probably be continuously or near ongoing. Moreover, you will approach the greater part of the training and anticipating data your specialist gives to genuine cash customers. When you sense that you're prepared for a genuine cash account you can change from a demo record to genuine assets.

Outline

There are a few stages you should take before you start executing in the forex advertise. You have to initially find out about the budgetary markets and the kind of data you can find out about preceding exchanging. Attempt to find out about both basic and specialized investigation. Discover a forex facilitate that you accept is dependable and gives a plenty of data. Ultimately, utilize a demo account before you start to chance genuine cash.

★ Forex Day Trading Risk Management

Every successful forex day trader manages their risk; it is one of, if not the, most crucial elements of ongoing profitability.

To start, you must keep your risk on each trade very small, and 1% or less is typical. This means if you have a $3,000 account, you shouldn't lose more than $30 on a single trade. That may seem small, but losses do add up, and even a good day-trading strategy will see strings of losses. Risk is managed using a stop-loss order, which will be discussed in the Scenario sections below.

Forex Day Trading Strategy

While a strategy can potentially have many components and can be analyzed for profitability in various ways, a strategy is often ranked based on its win-rate and risk/reward ratio.

Win Rate

Your win rate represents the number of trades you win out a given total number of trades. Say you win 55 out of 100 trades, your win rate is 55 percent. While it isn't required, having a win rate above 50 percent is ideal for most day traders, and 55 percent is acceptable and attainable.

Risk/Reward

Risk/reward signifies how much capital is being risked attaining a certain profit. If a trader loses 10 pips on losing trades but makes 15 on winning trades, she is making more on the winners than she's losing on losers. This means that even if the trader only wins 50% of her trades, she will be profitable. Therefore, making more on winning trades is also a strategic component for which many forex day traders strive.

A higher win rate for trades means more flexibility with your risk/reward, and a high risk/reward means your win rate can be lower and you'd still be profitable.

Hypothetical Scenario

Assume a trader has $5,000 in capital funds, and they have a decent win rate of 55% on their trades. They risk only 1% of their capital or $50 per trade. This is accomplished by using a stop-loss order. For this scenario, a stop-loss order is placed 5 pips away from the trade entry price, and a target is placed 8 pips away.

This means that the potential reward for each trade is 1.6 times greater than the risk (8/5). Remember, you want winners to be bigger than losers.

While trading a forex pair for two hours during an active time of day it's usually possible to make about five round turn trades (round turn includes entry and exit) using the above parameters. If there are 20 trading days in a month, the trader is making 100 trades, on average, in a month.

Trading Leverage

Forex brokers provide leverage up to 50:1 (more in some countries). For this example, assume the trader is using 30:1 leverage, as usually that is more than enough leverage for forex day traders. Since the trader has $5,000, and leverage is 30:1, the trader is able to take positions worth up to $150,000. Risk is still based on the original $5,000; this keeps the risk limited to a small portion of the deposited capital.

Forex brokers often don't charge a commission, but rather increase the spread between the bid and ask, thus making it more difficult to day trade profitably. ECN brokers offer a very small spread, making it easier to trade profitably, but they typically charge about $2.50 for every $100,000 traded ($5 round turn).

Trading Currency Pairs

If you're day trading a currency pair like the GBP/USD, you can risk $50 on each trade, and each pip of movement is worth $10 with a standard lot (100,000 units worth of currency). Therefore you can take a position of one standard lot with a 5-pip stop-loss order, which will keep the risk of loss to $50 on the trade. That also means a winning trade is worth $80 (8 pips x $10).

This estimate can show how much a forex day trader could make in a month by executing 100 trades:

- 55 trades were profitable: 55 x $80 = $4,400
- 45 trades were losers: 45 x ($50) = ($2,250)

Gross profit is $4,400 - $2,250 = $2,150 if no commissions (win rate would likely be lower though)

Net profit is $2,150 - $500 = $1,650 if using a commission broker (win rate would be like be higher though)

Assuming a net profit of $1,650, the return on the account for the month is 33 percent ($1,650/$5,000). This may seem very high, and it is a very good return. See Refinements below to see how this return may be affected.

Slippage Larger Than Expected Loss

It won't always be possible to find five good day trades each day, especially when the market is moving very slowly for extended periods.

Slippage is an inevitable part of trading. It results in a larger loss than expected, even when using a stop-loss order. It's common in very fast-moving markets.

To account for slippage in the calculation of your potential profit, reduce the net profit by 10% (this is a high estimate for slippage, assuming you avoid holding through major economic data releases). This would reduce the net profit potential generated by your $5,000 trading capital to $1,485 per month.

You can adjust the scenario above based on your typical stop loss and target, capital, slippage, win rate, position size, and commission parameters.

To Cover UP:-

This simple risk-controlled strategy indicates that with a 55% win rate, and making more on winners than you lose on losing trades, it's possible to attain returns north of 20% per month with forex day trading. Most traders shouldn't expect to make this much; while it sounds simple, in reality, it's more difficult.

Even so, with a decent win rate and risk/reward ratio, a dedicated forex day trader with a decent strategy can make between 5% and 15% a month thanks to leverage. Also remember, you don't need much capital to get started; $500 to $1,000 is usually enough.

How to Read a Forex Quote

Currencies are always quoted in pairs, such as GBP/USD or USD/JPY. The reason they are quoted in pairs is because, in every foreign exchange transaction, you are simultaneously buying one currency and selling another.

Here is an example of a foreign exchange rate for the British pound versus the U.S. dollar:

GBP / USD = 1.32448

(Base Currency)   (Quote Currency)

The first listed currency to the left of the slash ("/") is known as the **base currency** (in this example, the British pound), while the second one on the right is called the **counter or quote currency** (in this example, the U.S. dollar).When buying, the exchange rate tells you how much you have to pay in units of the quote currency to buy **ONE unit of the base currency**. In the example above, you have to pay 1.51258 U.S. dollars to buy 1 British pound. When selling, the exchange rate tells you how many units of the quote currency you get for selling **ONE unit of the base currency**. In the example above, you will receive 1.51258 U.S. dollars when you sell 1 British pound.

The base currency is the "basis" for the buy or the sell.

If you buy EUR/USD this simply means that you are buying the base currency and simultaneously selling the quote currency. In caveman talk, "buy EUR, sell USD." You would *buy* the pair if you believe the base currency will appreciate (gain value) relative to the quote currency. You would *sell* the pair if you think the base currency will depreciate (lose value) relative to the quote currency.

Long/Short

First, you should determine whether you want to **buy** or **sell**. If you want to buy (which actually means buy the base currency and sell the quote currency), you want the base currency to rise in value and then you would sell it back at a higher price.

In trader talk, this is called "going long" or taking a "long position." Just remember: **long = buy.**

If you want to sell (which actually means sell the base currency and buy the quote currency), you want the base currency to fall in value and then you would buy it back at a lower price. This is called "going short" or taking a "short position". Just remember: **short = sell.**

The Bid, Ask and Spread

All forex quotes are quoted with two prices: the **bid** and **ask**. In general, the **bid** is lower than the **ask** price. The **bid** is the price at which your broker is willing to *buy* the base currency in exchange for the quote currency.

This means the bid is the best available price at which you (the trader) will sell to the market. If you want to sell something, the broker will buy it from you at the bid price.

The **ask** is the price at which your broker will *sell* the base currency in exchange for the quote currency.

This means the ask price is the best available price at which you will buy from the market. Another word for ask is the **offer price.** If you want to buy something, the broker will sell (or offer) it to you at the ask price.

The difference between the bid and the ask price is known as the **SPREAD**.

On the EUR/USD quote above, the bid price is 1.34568 and the ask price is 1.34588. Look at how this broker makes it so easy for you to trade away your money.

If you want to sell EUR, you click "Sell" and you will sell euros at 1.34568.If you want to buy EUR, you click "Buy" and you will buy euros at 1.34588.

★STOCK MARKET

The stock exchange, or values showcase as it is likewise known, is one of the world's most prevalent and effectively exchanged budgetary markets. It's additionally a spot where numerous individuals go to attempt to profit, both rapidly and over the long haul. There are numerous approaches to profit in the financial exchange, utilizing both conventional strategies and some increasingly imaginative techniques.

What Are Stocks?

Responsibility for in fact speaks to the proprietorship, or if nothing else halfway possession, of organizations. Proprietors of stocks in many nations have a lawful right to cast a ballot at organization investors' gatherings and will get a notice when the gatherings are held. After offers are given by organizations, they can be (and typically are) exchanged progressively on the optional market.

There are a few different ways to profit with the buy, possession and closeout of stock in the financial exchange:

Development Stocks

Stocks whose organizations are relied upon to encounter solid development are known as development stocks. One of the fundamental ways brokers can profit with them is holding their offers until they increment in cost, and after that offering them to take a benefit (also called a capital addition). Some of the time, share costs will change uncontrollably in unpredictable markets, offering dealers chances to purchase, sell and take benefits quickly.

Initial public offering

At the point when organizations first issue offers to general society, they hold beginning open contributions (IPOs) to permit first buy rights to potential purchasers. A few IPOs are intently viewed and vigorously exchanged. That is on the grounds that stock costs from promising new organizations can be offered up rapidly from low levels to exceptionally significant levels in a brief timeframe. This produces open doors for snappy and once in a while soak profits.

Value Stocks

As the name proposes, esteem stocks are those that are underestimated by the market, displaying a decent can foresee potential purchasers. Worth contributing can require intensive examination of an organization's budget reports to comprehend its monetary wellbeing and future potential, yet this might merit the exertion.

Acclaimed financial specialist Warren Buffett is one surely understood advocate of significant worth contributing. Roused by the worth contributing procedures of contributing theoretician Benjamin Graham, Buffett had the option to store up a fortune searching out underestimated stocks over a time of quite a while. Graham accepted that stocks spoke to a decent arrangement when they were estimated at 66% or less of their "natural" value.

Income Stocks

Holding salary stocks is a conventional method to profit in the financial exchange. Loads of organizations that acquire strong incomes regularly pay profits, more often than not on a quarterly premise, to investors. Stocks that pay generally higher profits, or salary stocks, can habitually profit for their proprietors. Be that as it may, dealers may frequently need to gather a lot of such stocks to get huge profit installments.

Stock Funds

Holding common assets, or trade exchanged assets, is another way that merchants can make cash on stocks. A reserve is comprised of a gathering of money related resources, frequently stocks, that are packaged all together security. Shared assets regularly require least buy sums and are not exchanged during business sector hours.

Trade exchanged assets are like shared assets, however are exchanged during business sector hours as though they were individual stocks and can be purchased and sold in littler additions than common assets. Both common assets and trade exchanged subsidizes that hold stocks frequently pay out profits from their possessions on a standard basis

Investment opportunities And Futures

The alternatives and fates markets are in fact not part of the securities exchanges, yet they can give great chances to profiting with stocks.

In alternatives exchanging, merchants can get the choice to purchase or sell a stock at a predetermined cost at a future lapse date. In the event that the securities exchange's cost is higher or lower than the choice's predefined strike cost at its termination date, at that point the holder of the choice can practice their purchasing or selling right and pocket the distinction between the two costs. Alternatives can likewise be purchased or sold on the auxiliary market before the termination date. Additionally, prospects agreements are sold for certain significant stock files and some individual stocks.

Prospects agreements are sold at an expected future cost for the list or stock. The agreements for the most part terminate four times each year, once close to the finish of each quarter. In the event that the stock or record worth is higher than the fates cost at termination, the purchaser of the agreement can take a benefit. On the off chance that the worth is lower, the vender of the agreement takes a profit.

Preferred Stock Vs. Common Stock

Stocks are generally given in two kinds: favored stock and normal stock. Normal investors, as referenced above, are given democratic rights. Favored investors don't have casting a ballot rights. In any case, favored stock more often than not gets higher profit installments than normal stock and has more noteworthy assurances of reimbursement should the organization default on some loans.

Some favored offers are likewise convertible into regular offers. These offers can be changed over at a predefined proportion. In the event that the cost of the convertible favored offers is lower than the cost of basic offers after the change rate is applied, the favored offers can be traded for normal offers at a benefit to the shareholder.

Short-Selling

Short-selling a stock is another basic method for profiting with stocks. While brokers frequently consider purchasing, or going "long," on stocks they think will ascend in an incentive as a manner to pick up cash, short-selling adopts the contrary strategy.

Short merchants obtain shares, ordinarily from their intermediary, so as to sell, or "short," stocks they think will fall in worth. After the offers fall in value, they repurchase them and return them to the moneylender. They pocket the distinction in the cost at which they sold the offers and the lower cost at which they got them back.

Stock Splits

Stock parts can on occasion be endorsed by organization sheets and investors. At the point when a stock split happens, the investor is conceded a different number of extra offers for each offer held, in proportions of 2-to-1, 3-to at least 1. The estimation of each offer is separated in a comparing way. Yet, when a split happens, the investor's potential future property of the organization, and comparing riches, might be helped significantly.

Summary

There are an assortment of approaches to profit in the securities exchange, and subsequently it is where numerous dealers go to look for formation of riches. Stocks, similar to any money related exchanging, can include potential dangers and misfortunes. Be that as it may, merchants may improve their odds by getting comfortable with the numerous roads wherein to utilize the financial exchange furthering their potential benefit.

Any sentiments, news, look into, examinations, costs, other data, or connections to outsider locales are given as general market critique and don't comprise venture counsel. FXCM won't acknowledge risk for any misfortune or harm including, without constraint, to any loss of benefit which may emerge legitimately or in a roundabout way from utilization of or dependence on such data.

★ Bitcoin

So you want to get your hands on some free bitcoin, eh? By now, you might have heard of how you can make money with bitcoin, magic internet money and digital currency that can be traded or used to make purchases. This digital money uses encryption to make safe and secure transactions instantly from anywhere in the world. Not regulated by any bank, government or Federal Reserve, this open network is managed by the users and investors themselves. Here is our guide to earning real money with bitcoin in 2019.

Contrary to people's knowledge, getting bitcoin is easy, there are a number of ways to earn bitcoin online- some more popular than the others. There are methods that involve a minimal effort with the minimal return and others more lucrative that requires you to have better expertise in the industry.
Below are some of the most famous ways to make money with bitcoin.

1.Mining bitcoin

No, you don't have to raise the ground to get bitcoin. Not in that sense anyway.
So, why do you call it mining? Similar to gold miners, bitcoin miners have to bring out the gold, in this case, bitcoin into the surface.
Did you dare to ask how? While paper money has a government, who prints and distributes it, Bitcoin has miners who use special software to solve math problems and are issued with bitcoin in exchange. This system is what makes the Bitcoin network go round.

Mining Bitcoin used to be relatively simple, and the earliest miners were able to mine thousands of Bitcoin using their home computers. However, in today's very competitive and volatile market, miners buy expensive computer parts, that the high street customer has little access to, required for more processing power in order to mine more difficult algorithms. Since this is a race who can solve blocks faster, miners team up in what we call mining pools where they combine their processing power in order to solve each transaction first. The reward mostly comes from several miners' fees, is then split up by members of the pool.

Remember that bitcoin mining is not as profitable as it used to and many are claiming it to be the end of profitable mining.

The future of mining in 2019 will depend on the price of Bitcoin. If the price goes up, mining will continue to evolve and the number of miners will increase. If the price goes down, miners will gradually disappear.an excerpt from 2miners' blog
It presents new miners with new challenges and also unique opportunities to come into the market when everyone else is leaving and then the price of bitcoin will go up. It all depends on your ability to analyze the market and correctly predict future changes.

instructions to profit with bitcoin , One of the most well known methods for how to benefit from Bitcoin will be Bitcoin mining. There can be two types of mining – your own, own mining or cloud mining.

In the event that you need to mine separately (which means, with your mining rig), it probably won't be the most ideal method for how to profit with Bitcoin. Bitcoin is viewed as one of the harder cryptographic forms of money to mine since it's a subject of standard achievement and many individuals need to pitch into the publicity, yet there's a restricted stockpile of it. A solitary apparatus, in the same class as it could be, might battle to create noteworthy benefits, particularly when you consider the power and support costs.

Cloud mining, in any case, has turned out to be prominent in the course of the most recent couple of years. It's an incredible elective with regards to mining since you don't have to purchase any equipment or programming, collect or even DO anything – you should simply pay a one-time expense for an agreement and that is it! For the most part, toward the finish of consistently, you'll get your income. The sum will be founded on your arrangement of decision and the power bill at the office that the cloud mining administration depends on.

Generally speaking, digital currency mining is a prevalent strategy for individuals looking on the most proficient method to profit with Bitcoin. It requires some learning and aptitude in the field to have the option to perform it effectively (particularly on the off chance that you need to manufacture your apparatus), however the exertion is unquestionably worth the outcomes.

2. Bitcoin Faucets

If you don't mind looking at a few ads and answering surveys, you can visit a bitcoin faucet website. Generally, these websites generate revenue from advertisements placed on their pages. Those who visit their site and answer short questions or captchas will be paid from the small portion of their revenue. You can readily check one of the most popular faucet sites here: earn.com.

3. Pay To Click (PTC) Websites

There are several websites that will pay you in bitcoin if you watch an ad or click to a certain page containing ads. If you are ad immune and want to make quick crypto buck–this can be a good idea. Bear in mind, to make any significant money is still very hard work and a rather tedious task. BTC4ADS pays around 100 satoshis (0.00000100 ฿) and Coinadder pays around 25 satoshis per click.

4. Doing Micro Jobs

Much like Microworkers and Cloudfactory, which pay you a small fee to complete very simple tasks like watching a YouTube video or completing someone's survey, there are several micro working sites that will pay you in bitcoin. Bitcoinget is the major player in this market which will pay you around 20,000 satoshis per task while there are several others like Cointasker that will pay you a slightly lower sum.

5. Writing about bitcoin

Cryptocurrency, in general, is a new niche and there is a scarcity of writers who genuinely know this niche. This means the market is flooded with newbie copywriters who simply rehash the content that contributes to the deterioration of quality. However, if you really know this niche and you have decent writing skills, you can actually make money.

CCN, Blockchain Aliens are among several websites that pay you for writing about bitcoin. You can also find a lot

of related jobs freelance websites like upwork and
freelancer.com

6. Help others, get tipped in bitcoin

You can also get tipped in bitcoin by helping other people.
One of the most notable platform to do so is bitfortip,
which tips bitcoin as an incentive for helping people.
Bitcoin is a new technology and there are people who are
genuinely passionate about it and excited about what is to
follow so incentives like this help to build a positive vibe
around the community and also help people solve their
problems.

7. Gambling bitcoin

Though its not advisable to anyone, if you are self-aware
enough, the bitcoin gambling market can still be a good
source of income. Just like any form of gambling, the
people in general always lose and the casinos always win
but since bitcoin gambling is a very little heard of the
term, you can get huge bonus for joining or even several
rounds of your stake to start with. Sites like Bitstarz and
mbit are major players in Crypto gambling business.

8. Buying and Holding

Start with creating a wallet to keep your bitcoin safe. There
are many places that allow you to do so. Paxful, for
example, provides a free digital wallet whenever you sign
up for an account. This is the easiest way if you are
planning on buying and holding bitcoin. Make sure that
the website you're using is a safe and reliable one.
Investing in Bitcoin is a waiting game of its value to rise.
This lets you decide when is a good time to buy or sell.

There are several factors that contribute to how bitcoin is valued and you never know what will trigger the next bear market.

"Hodl", a term the Bitcoin community whenever they are holding their coin with the belief their coin will be profitable one day. The slang word earned the backronym "Hold On for Dear Life" in the cryptocurrency space.

Note that this method can be tricky so don't take anyone's advice about it. Research and learn about Bitcoin and come up to your own conclusion.

9. Running a signature campaign in Bitcoin Talk forum

Bitcointalk is one of the oldest bitcoin forum set up by Satoshi Nakamoto himself. This is probably the most popular forum in crypto sphere and used by millions of people. If you are an avid follower of the forum and you have racked up some authority from consistent posting, then your posts of bitcointalk will have a sponsored signature and you'll get paid by sponsors for every post you make on the forum.

According to Steemit, you can easily make a bit of coin doing simple forum posting – for example, a full member can earn 0.0003 btc per post

10. Bitcoin Trading

There is potential to make big money trading bitcoin. Unlike buying and holding, trading bitcoin means you buy at a low price and sell them back at a higher price. This requires practice and knowledge of the market and to some extent a crystal ball. Given that the cryptocurrency market is extremely volatile, this method can be very risky.

"There is money in Arbitrage"
The volatile nature of the market, however, gives rise to the opportunities for arbitrage. Arbitrage–as per Investopedia is the simultaneous buying and selling of securities, currency, or commodities in different markets or in derivative forms in order to take advantage of differing prices for the same asset.

There are several reasons why bitcoin arbitrage takes place, Market demands, the difference in the quality of the markets and diversity in client behaviors to name a few. If you have a good knowledge of the market and you can keep surveillance over multiple exchanges spanning over multiple countries, there is a good chance of making a big profit margin.

If you have at least some technical knowledge, you can also profit from using arbitrage bots.

Profit Strategy using bitcoin bots arbitrage
Day trading has a good profit margin if done correctly
Though bitcoin is getting less volatile by day, we should not forget that its still early adoption years and there was price fluctuations of more than 3% in a single minute as early as April 2018. Day trading has a lower risk than say "hodling" but also lower rewards unless you are investing heavily. But if you are prepared to do your research on the bitcoin market and rules of economics in general, you can come up with your own strategies to profit from day trading without sacrificing too much.

11. Accepting Bitcoin as a means of payment

Bitcoin is, after all, a digital currency. So why not sell goods or services in exchange for bitcoin. This gives you the freedom to sell anything to anyone without going through any banks or financial institutions that may prevent you to do so. If you are already selling, why not accept bitcoin as payment. As a matter of fact, there is a massive list of businesses that are already accepting bitcoin.

These are some ways in which you can earn money with bitcoin. If you choose to mine or invest, it is important to do as much research as possible and be prepared for all possible outcomes.

12. Lending bitcoin

The decentralized nature of bitcoin and other cryptocurrencies make it simpler to make transactions without needing authorities to validate it. In such a case, you can also loan bitcoin to potential loaners at a certain interest rate. It is also a very good alternative to "hodling" as you are actually making use of the wealth rather than keep it unmoved and it's better for the economy in general. Several lend-and-borrow platforms like Unchained Capital, Bitbond and BTCpop allow you to lend your bitcoin for interest rate up to 15%.

Bear in mind that this is still a new market and there are hustlers who may try to cheat you. Always choose trustworthy platforms and loaners while making your investments.

13. Binary Trading with bitcoin

Binary trading's have existed in the financial world for a very long time and did not take long enough to make a journey for that financial scheme to migrate to the crypto world. Binary—as the name suggests has just two options, a trader purchases an option and at the expiration time, the trader either is either "in the money" or "out of the money". In its true essence, its not too much further from gambling or Russian roulette.

All you have to do is make an investment on an option. Say there are two options to invest– for the bitcoin price of $3000 now (at 10 AM), you can either invest in the price will be more than $3000 by 6 PM or the price will be less than $3000 by 6 PM. If at 5 PM the bitcoin is indeed higher than $3000, you earn the payout of certain payout percentage of your investment, if it's lower, you lose your investment. Another option is to "put" if you think the price of BTC will go down. If the price at the expiration time is lower than the original price, you earn the option's payout.

Remember its plain gambling and nothing to do with intricacies of bitcoin or other cryptos in any way. Nonetheless, its still a way to make money with bitcoin though its highly inadvisable.

14. Make money with Bitcoin Affiliates

Affiliate marketing works when you generate sales leads for a product or a service and the organization offering a product or service pays you certain commission for bringing in potential consumers who would otherwise not have been interested.

Usually, these 3 steps allow you to set up your own affiliate business for passive income:

Sign up for the affiliate program as an affiliate marketer. When you are accepted as a marketer, you will receive a unique URL that has a link to their product or service but also has a unique identifier which means they keep a record of who sent them there.

You then share that link on any web or social media platform(Website, Facebook, Twitter etc.) When someone comes to visit the website through your link and makes a purchase, you get a certain percentage as your affiliate fee. We at Paxful also have an amazing affiliate program where you get paid 50% of the bitcoin escrow fee from your direct affiliate and 10% of the escrow fee from the affiliates made by your affiliates.

15. Being a Master node

Bitcoin is usually used as an umbrella term for all the cryptocurrencies and though experts would say the return for being a bitcoin master node is not all that profitable, you can still serve as a master node for several other cryptocurrencies and get a reward for your service to the blockchain.

Master node is a dedicated node that keeps track of blockchain in real-time. Much like bitcoin full nodes, they are always up and running.

In addition to saving, validating and announcing valid transactions to other nodes, master nodes also perform other tasks with the blockchain including ensuring smooth protocol operations, governing voting events etc Next to validating, saving and broadcasting transactions, master nodes sometimes also facilitate other events on the blockchain-dependent on their nature, such as governing voting events etc. For their dedicated service, they are heavily incentivized. It typically depends on the type of cryptocurrency but Dash, PIVX, Blocknet, Stakenet and Zcoin are the 5 major coins that have the best incentives for a master node.

Tips for making more profit with bitcoin

Needed to say, here are a few tips before you start earning money through bitcoin.

Like having physical cash, keep your bitcoin safe and keep your bitcoin wallet safe. This may mean enabling your Google 2FA, backing up your device or keeping your antivirus updated. There are a lot of digital threats waiting for you.

The industry is prone to fluctuations. This can be a good thing when you stay on top of it and learn the risk that comes with it.

Keep in mind that there is no free Bitcoin. Although there are several methods to earn from it. With the market always growing, there will always be a demand in expertise or a new product that will develop with time.

More about Bitcoin:-

Bitcoin, as a digital currency, has been dependent upon standard discussion for a long while now. Individuals investigate its past and theorize about its future for a wide assortment of reasons – a few people need to know the historical backdrop of cryptographic forms of money, others are interested about conceivable venture openings. Whatever your explanation would be, in this guide we'll discuss various methods for how to profit with Bitcoin.

We'll discuss the various methods for how to benefit from Bitcoin – yet most importantly, we'll contemplate on why Bitcoin is so prominent in any case. At that point, when we comprehend the history (or if nothing else its overly short form) of this present digital currency's development and ascend to control, we will investigate its benefitting openings.

] The Short Version of Bitcoin History

] The Fall of Bitcoin

] How to profit with Bitcoin?

] Buying Bitcoin

] Investing

The Short Version of Bitcoin History

Bitcoin was made in 2009 by somebody (or some gathering of individuals) known by the nom de plume Satoshi Nakamoto. At the time that it came around, no one had even known about digital currencies, not to mention experienced one.

Bitcoins newborn child and high school years were truly harsh – it neglected to increase noteworthy footing and consideration, despite the fact that its costs varied for what (around then) appeared to be a considerable amount. Nobody was all the while considering how to profit with Bitcoin.

At last, toward the start of 2017 Bitcoin broke the benchmark of $1000. In simply a question of a year, it figured out how to nearly come to the $20,000 checkmark. Obviously, this was tremendous – everyone either remained with their jawlines arriving at the floor or emptied all that they had into Bitcoin – it appeared to be a relentless power that continued expanding its energy each and every day. In the event that you've as of late checked the Bitcoin value graphs, in any case, you realize that things went in a new direction.

The Fall of Bitcoin

Toward the start of 2018, Bitcoin's cost was around $11,000, at that point arrived at a stunning low of nearly $6000. At the hour of composing this guide, Bitcoin is at present worth $6400. So… How to profit with Bitcoin?

What caused an accident of this greatness? Indeed, there are numerous theories.

Individuals who frequently see how to profit with cryptographic money will presumably realize what the Bitcoin value diagram resembles:

step by step instructions to profit with bitcoin - diagram

Does it, maybe, help you to remember something? A… tooth, possibly?

This sort of outline is known as a "shark tooth" graph. It implies that a digital currency's (for this situation – Bitcoin's) value rose and fell so quick that the way it took on the diagram looks like a sharp shark tooth.

This is likewise called a "burst bubble". A celebrated financial specialist was even cited saying that Bitcoin was the "greatest air pocket burst ever". Purposes for this are estimated to be the developed publicity, absence of help for the blockchain, advertise controls and many, some more.

Whatever the case may be, clearly if nothing else, Bitcoin took a colossal jump from which it is as of now attempting to recoup. Anyone seeing how to profit with Bitcoin ought to presumably remember these things.

How to profit with Bitcoin?

So since you know a few things about the ascent and fall of Bitcoin, we can at long last move into the lucrative techniques.

There are many techniques to profit with the assistance of Bitcoin, however in this guide, I'll spread only the fundamental ones – in the event that I needed to show them all, this guide would be in any event 300 pages in length.

The rundown isn't formed in a particular request. A few techniques work better (or quicker) than others, however – for the most part – it relies upon the individual.

Buying Bitcoin

No, I'm not kidding.

There are gigantic gatherings of individuals who "contribute" into Bitcoin by essentially getting it. This is a dangerous strategy, obviously, yet most likely the least difficult one to perform.

There are two or three kinds of such speculators. A few people simply purchase a specific amount of the coin and forget about it for a year… or ten. These individuals typically have no genuine expectation to benefit present moment – they regularly put stock in the effective eventual fate of digital forms of money and expectation that their venture currently will one day present to them a ten times benefit.

Another kind of Bitcoin financial specialists are the individuals who do heaps of research, read the majority of the accessible expectations on the most proficient method to profit with digital currency and go through weeks breaking down information and insights. These individuals will in general have a quite certain time span as a main priority – more often than not, they are hoping to contribute present moment and simply need to realize when to do it. Additionally, these ventures will in general be littler when contrasted with the long haul ones – all things considered, individuals contribute having done a huge amount of research previously, yet in the event that their speculation fizzles, they could simply proceed onward to whenever outline.

In case you're contemplating how to profit with Bitcoin or how to profit with cryptographic money when all is said in done, purchasing Bitcoin can be an extraordinary starter – or a grievous one. It can profit genuine quick or might drive you to the edge of obligation. Everything relies upon one single factor – the measure of research you've done already.

Investing

What's more, no, not the purchasing bitcoin-and afterward selling-it sort of contributing.

There are many decisions you have with regards to putting resources into Bitcoin. You could profit with Bitcoin by putting resources into new businesses, organizations, stocks or even blockchain advancement itself.

Blockchain-based new businesses are an exceptionally famous decision with regards to putting resources into a digital currency related field. Effectively, some eminent new companies have made it into the standard achievement (for example Daring's Basic Attention Token). You would need to do some uncovering and locate the following best thing, however on the off chance that you'd be correct and put resources into the startup while it's still in its beginning of earliest stages, you may very well cashed in big and develop your benefits to the rooftop.

Organizations that manage Bitcoin or blockchain advancement (or research) are additionally a decent choice for speculations. You'd need to investigate their information – White Paper, their objectives and hard working attitudes, results, insights, and so on., and if their general view appears to be appealing, you could consider putting resources into their activities or the organization itself.

You ought to be cautious with ventures, however – particularly with regards to digital forms of money. Its a well known fact that the cryptographic money market is a truly capricious spot. Continuously get your work done and inquire about the articles that you intend to put into, or else the topic of "how to profit with Bitcoin?" may transform into "how to escape obligation (no Bitcoin)?".

✦ Cryptocurrency

You will adapt precisely how to make cash exchanging altcoins

2017 was a major year for digital currency, however it's still early days.

… And now everybody's searching for the following Bitcoin.

To enable you to find precisely how to make cash exchanging altcoins – without taking a chance with your entire speculation.

1. What Are Altcoins?

Altcoins are essentially simply some other cryptographic money separated from Bitcoin. Presently while Bitcoin is the most notable cryptographic money, there's still more than 2,000 altcoins available – and the greater part of them aren't anyplace close as well known.

Also, more alternatives = increasingly potential exchanging benefits.

Here's some ongoing instances of digital forms of money that have expanded by 1,000+ percent in just 24 hours…

Be that as it may, this isn't just about profiting!

Altcoins offer heaps of advantages – as you you'll find underneath…

2. 7 Reasons Why You Should Learn How To Make Money Trading Altcoins

1 You needn't bother with a great deal of cash.

Regardless of whether you start off contributing just $100, you can in any case make good comes back with the intensity of self multiplying dividends. Which leads me to my next point…

2 The profits are absurd.
100% gains in a day? 1,000% in a month? When you figure out how to make cash exchanging altcoins, these sorts of increases are entirely achieveable – which overwhelms the profits you'll see on most customary ventures.

3 Cryptocurrency is what's to come.

While there might be an air pocket at the present time, digital money is an amazingly troublesome innovation. That is to say, digital currency could actually change the eventual fate of cash! Protection, online security, obscurity, everyday installments – these are only a couple of the ways altcoins could change our reality. Exchanging digital currency resembles picking the following Apple, Amazon or Tesla!

4 Altcoins are blasting at the present time
. Since the brilliant ascent of Bitcoin, there will never be been a superior time to put resources into cryptographic forms of money. What's more, I completely expect altcoin exchanging to blast in 2018.

5 It's enjoyable.
The cosmic highs. The sensational lows. The 1,000% increases… Is there much else fun than the rush of riding the cryptographic money wave?

Evidently, there's a LOT of hazard with regards to altcoins – yet that is a piece of the ride. Simply make sure to contribute capably.

6 It's anything but difficult to begin.

It may take two or three days to get confirmed on Coinbase (where a great many people purchase their Bitcoin) – however once you're in, you're in. You needn't bother with any understanding, capabilities or huge cash to get included.

3. Instructions to Make Money Trading Altcoins.

A little tip:
Take as much time as necessary and don't race through the means beneath!
It's essential to look into your altcoins throroughly, comprehend the dangers and think cautiously before you place any exchanges.

Presently immediately, here's the means by which to make cash exchanging altcoins in 7 basic advances.

1. Sign Up To Coinbase.

Before you can start exchanging altcoins, you have to purchase Bitcoin.
A great many people get their Bitcoin from Coinbase – it's a snappy, simple approach to get it on the web.

2. Move Your Money To An Exchange.

You can exchange altcoins at trades – two of the most prevalent are Bittrex and Binance. Trades are the place most major altcoins are recorded – they're just a spot where you can purchase and sell crypto on the web, kinda like eBay for cryptographic money!

3. Waitlist Your Altcoins.
Presently I realize what you're thinking…
When there's a great many altcoins to look over, how would you realize which is ideal? By and by, I'd suggest searching for a long haul altcoin that you wouldn't see any problems with holding for a half year or more – just in the event that the market changes.

4. Contribute.
Keep in mind: costs are unpredictable to the point that they can change from moment to minute by a couple of percent…
So I'd suggest hanging tight for a plunge in the market before you put resources into your top pick. These plunges will in general happen at regular intervals in the middle of high development spurts.
You can watch out for the most recent digital currency costs

5. Screen Your Gains.
Trades like Bittrex or Binance make it simple to follow your benefits/misfortunes.
Also, when costs are fluctuating so quickly, it gets a brief period devouring to continually figure costs.
Rather, introduce the Blockfolio application.

Blockfolio refreshes your digital currency portfolio every time you open it – and it's really simple to utilize as well.

6. Sell Up When You're Ready.

So how would you realize when you're prepared to sell?
Set benefit targets – and when you hit them, sell out.
At the point when you're figuring out how to make cash exchanging altcoins, it's anything but difficult to become overly enthusiastic with voracity. Be that as it may, don't let occur! Since when costs are so unstable, if something goes up, it'll in all likelihood shoot down as well. What's more, this typically occurs all of a sudden! So sell up and get out when you hit your benefit limits.

Note: a great many people exchange their altcoins over into BTC when they're prepared to sell out.

7. Money Out.

Keep in mind: You haven't made anything until you money out. Of course, those 100% increases are extraordinary... In any case, they don't mean anything until the cash is in your bank!
So just move your parity back to Coinbase – and afterward money them out into your ledger. It may take two or three days for the cash to come through.

4. Data Is Everything.

At the point when you're figuring out how to make cash exchanging altcoins, you can take a brazen easy route!
… You see, I'm no exchange examiner.
… I don't try to be one.
… And I'm ridiculous horrendous at maths!

Be that as it may, you don't have to understand diagrams or ace numbers to figure out how to make cash exchanging altcoins.
All you need is the capacity to inquire about.
Since data = benefits. Each time there's another update, official statement or enormous declaration, you'll find that the costs of altcoins change pretty quickly. So join some Facebook gatherings. Peruse some ICO white papers. Sweep through the most recent digital currency news on Reddit.

What's more, discover all that you can about your ventures.

8. Data Pays Off.

As of late, I made generally 90% on Bitcoin Cash the day preceding it was recorded on Coinbase…
In any case, I had no aim of selling up until I got a tip off that Bitcoin Cash was going to crash! Soon after, heaps of venders dumped it in a major frenzy sell.

Quick forward 24 hours and Bitcoin Cash has dropped by 70%! Perceive how significant data is presently?

Proven Altcoin Trading Strategies

1. Slow, Compound Interest Gains.

On the off chance that you don't extravagant exchanging the high hazard, unstable altcoins – don't stress!

Rather, just spotlight on making a little rate increase regular. 10% a day may appear to be moderate, however it develops speedy with accumulated dividends.

For instance, in the event that you made 10% premium every day for 25 days, you'd twofold your venture! Test out what you could gain with progressive accrual here.

What's more, that is very feasible with altcoins yet it does a ton of training and specialized learning.

2. HODL.

Discover a cryptographic money you can stay with longterm and essentially hold it.

It's basic AF. In any case, it likewise has exactly the intended effect!

On the off chance that you'd held Bitcoin since January 2017, you would have made a fortune. Furthermore, in the event that you put resources into a legitimate altcoin that has an extraordinary future, at that point the circumstance is the same.

Need a few hints? Look at my rundown of the best cryptographic forms of money to put resources into for 2018.

3. Pursue The Hype.

With regards to exchanging altcoins, your opposition isn't very keen.

You're not contending with Wall Street... Or banks... Or especially refined programming. When it comes to altcoins, you're basically simply exchanging a market brimming with regular person's hoping to acquire a speedy buck.

So while Bitcoin is being savaged by Wall Street, altcoins haven't hit the standard market. They're just facilitated on trades – which means you're not going up against numerous star level merchants... yet!

4. Exchanging Altcoins Comes With A Lot Of Risk.

With enormous returns comes greater duties!

What's more, with regards to figuring out how to make cash exchanging altcoins, a tremendous piece of the game is dealing with the potential dangers.

Keep in mind:
You're supporting your ventures on amazingly new innovation. Nobody realizes what the genuine worth is...

You likewise should be amazingly cautious about the trades you use. Some are superior to other people – so take care with which one you use.

Be careful about programmers, keep your login subtleties secure and consistently utilize twofold layer confirmation for you.

5. New kid on the block Trading Mistakes To Avoid.

Getting eager. In case you're making great returns, take some of it out in any event! When you're earning substantial sums of money, it's anything but difficult to give eagerness a chance to dominate. In any case, that will just damage you over the long haul...

Never contribute beyond what you can stand to lose. Principle #1 with regards to a contributing. Be dependable and don't go out on a limb.

FUD. FUD = dread, vulnerability and uncertainty. Facebook gatherings are a portion of the most exceedingly terrible for this stuff. Settle on certain choices and stick to them – in light of the fact that nobody comprehends what's on the horizon.

FOMO. Seen an altcoin that is hopped 1,000% in a day? Kindly don't pursue it! The dread of passing up a major opportunity can transform any prepared genius into a credulous new kid on the block. Rather, sit tight for the following open door as opposed to pursuing soaked purchases.

Siphon and dumps. In case you're new to the game, a siphon and dump is the point at which the cost of an altcoin is expanded by a gathering of merchants. It's essentially a trick that you can leave you holding low quality coins. On the off chance that you need assistance recognizing a siphon and dump, read this.

Imbecilic cash. Many low quality altcoins are flooding the market at the present time, and that is just going to deteriorate in 2018. So be cautious who you contribute with and consistently do your own examination.

Set stop misfortunes. With regards to altcoin exchanging, the market can crash really damn rapidly. So ensure your increases and set stop-misfortunes – these will sell your altcoins naturally if they drop by a sensational rate.

Try not to freeze. While exchanging altcoins, I've made $1,000 in my rest – however I've additionally lost comparative sums.

Best Crypto Currency Exchanegs for AltCoins to Buy/Sell Crypto Assets

Gradually and relentlessly, Bitcoin and altcoins are getting consideration from more speculators all around the globe.

What's more, why not? These digital forms of money are on numerous occasions demonstrating themselves to be a place of refuge against the administration's inflationary strategies.

That is the reason a few people are in any event, winning enthusiasm on crypto, while some are doing unadulterated hypothesis with momentary exchanging (for example purchase low, sell high).

What's more, we should not disregard the individuals who are simply beginning by glancing around to discover the response to questions like:

- Where do I purchase such monetary forms?
- What are the best digital currency trades?

In any case, before we talk about the best trades out there, I have to reveal to you that it's not very late to get put resources into cryptographic forms of money. At the hour of this composition, the Bitcoin and altcoin market is at an untouched high, with a market top of $219 billion. I accept we will cross the $300 billion imprint not long from now.

So since you realize you ought to contribute, here's the place you have to go to do that.

Note: This rundown is beginning from simple to utilize trades and moving towards a portion of the propelled trades.

8 Best Cryptocurrency Exchanges for Trading Cryptocurrency

1. Coinbase

Coinbase is a U.S. based crypto trade that serves the worldwide crowd. They are apprentice inviting and offers incredible speed and dependability.

Utilizing CoinBase you can rapidly purchase cryptographic forms of money and exchange simultaneously. They have an application for the two iOS and Android, which gives you the solace of trading digital forms of money from anyplace.

The security standard of CoinBase is truly elevated and they have been around for a long time. CoinBase is upheld in practically all the mainland (Africa, Asia Australia, Europe, North America, South America)

Coinbase likewise underpins well known stable coins, for example, DAI, USDC which is a significant part of any mainstream digital money trade.

2: Binance

Binance is a quickly developing trade that closed its ICO on 21st July 2017 and raised 15,000,000 USD. The organization is enlisted in Malta which is the crypto paradise and offers a blasting quick trade.

Since its ICO to till date, it has developed hugely and is currently put in top 10 digital money trades on the planet. It currently has more than 190 altcoins recorded on it which are just expanding as the days are passing.

Binance being a brought together trade has taken a one of a kind take to extend its business and furthermore gives a fair rebate to informal investors on the off chance that they use BNB coins. BNB is Binance Coin which is the local cash of this stage.

Peruse: Binance Review: Features, Fees in 2019 (Beginner's Guide)

Binance's charge structure is likewise one of a kind. To begin with they have 0.1% standard exchanging charge which is as of now very not exactly different friends. You can even decrease your charge further on the off chance that you pay your exchanging expense BNB as indicated by the underneath demonstrated structure.

To begin with Binance you have to enroll utilizing your email ID and the procedure is very basic and quick. Binance is one of only a handful couple of trades that offers versatile application for iOS and Android.

Being utilizing it for some time, I see it as too simple to even think about trading digital money while moving. You can watch this video to figure out how to utilize their versatile application.

They likewise have forceful plans like multi-lingual help, versatile applications for the two iOS and Android clients, Binance Angel Program, and the Community Coin Per Month and so forth for more reception of their foundation.

Make a record on Binance (Instant enactment) If you want to create Trade on Binance then click on this link to register in Binance:-
https://www.binance.com/en/markets?ref=35230773

3: BITMEX

BitMex is high volume crypto trade made by a gifted group of financial specialists, high-recurrence dealers and web designers for the crypto network.

Here you will never discover any issues with respect to the liquidity of your cryptographic forms of money.

The essential cash exchanged on this trade is Bitcoin and its future agreements.

Aside from Bitcoin contracts, one can likewise play around with future agreements for altcoins, for example, Bitcoin Cash, Ethereum, Cardano, Litecoin, Ripple.

The enrollment procedure on BitMex is very basic where you simply need to enlist through your email ID and their expense structure is additionally very direct as demonstrated as follows:

4: KuCoin

KuCoin is another simple and bother free cryptographic money trade. KuCoin offers numerous famous and one of a kind coin, for example, DragonChain, $KCS, and numerous others. Much the same as Binance, they offer a completely utilitarian portable application for Android and iOS.

To begin with KuCoin, you can store any crypto of your decision ex: BTC and start exchanging.

5:Changelly

Changelly is perhaps the most effortless approaches to get tightly to different cryptographic forms of money.

Changelly has a demonstrated reputation of reliably great items being put out into the crypto-space.

Perhaps the best thing about Changelly is that you don't have to experience any long confirmation or enlistment process. You simply sign in with your email ID (or any email ID) and start trading!

At present, it underpins in excess of 35 cryptographic forms of money alongside fiat matches, for example, USD/EUR. It is truly outstanding and most effortless to utilize trades out there. On the off chance that you need to know more, look at Harsh's audit on Changelly.

At the point when you use Changelly to trade digital money, Changelly bots associate continuously to probably the best and busiest cryptographic money trades in the market to get you the best cost.

More often than not, when utilizing Changelly, a crypto-to-crypto trade takes 5 to 30 minutes.

They charge a commission expense of 0.5% on each exchange, which I believe is negligible in return for the unpredictability and hazard that they bear in the interest of their clients.

Notwithstanding the commission, an excavator's charge is additionally paid by the client and is deducted legitimately from their crypto balance.

Be that as it may, all you need so as to purchase from Changelly is a VISA/MasterCard (credit/ charge card) or any Changelly-upheld cryptographic money and a wallet where you need to get your new coins.

The methodology is straightforward.

Head toward Changelly, and pursue the means given in this guide.

Note: Though this guide tells the best way to purchase Ripple in return for BTC, the procedure is actually the equivalent to purchase some other Changelly-bolstered digital currency.

Also, in the event that you need to purchase cryptos utilizing a VISA/MasterCard, at that point here is their official bit by bit control on doing that. (Despite the fact that this guide is for purchasing BTC utilizing a VISA/MasterCard, the procedure is equivalent to purchasing some other Changelly-bolstered digital money.)

6: HOUBI

Huobi Pro is a universal digital money trade that began in China however now has moved over the world to serve a most extreme number of speculators. It is based out of Singapore and has been working in this space effectively throughout the previous five years.

At this very moment, it involves the #3 spot on CoinMarketCap's rundown of trades by volume and has 244 cryptographic money sets. Subsequently, obviously, of this, you will never confront liquidity issues on this trade.

They additionally have versatile applications for both Android and iOS for clients who need to exchange cryptos in a hurry.

Their enrollment procedure is additionally quite basic and direct, so feel free to do the needful. Gracious, and to make sure you know, the trade expense is likewise truly low. Have a great time.

Do peruse, Huobi Exchange Review and Benefits of HT token: Can It Pull Off Another Binance?

7: BITTREX

Bittrex is a US-based cryptographic money trade that gives you the choice to exchange in excess of 190 digital currencies one after another. They are well-managed and agreeable with the majority of the present US rules, so crypto clients need not stress over the security of their assets.

Bittrex handles one of the biggest BTC exchanging volumes out of the considerable number of trades on the planet.

Here, the clients (purchasers/merchants) choose the rates wherein they need to exchange, and Bittrex charges them a little assistance expense for giving this stage (0.25%).

To begin with Bittrex, you have to enlist and sign in through your email ID, however to pull back assets, you have to do a KYC by presenting your ID archives and telephone number, just as empowering two-factor verification for higher cutoff points.

In any case, one beneficial thing about Bittrex is the record confirmation happens very quick.

Bittrex bolsters two sorts of records:

- Basic Account – withdrawal subsidizes worth up to 3 BTC/day.

- Advanced Account – withdrawal supports worth up to 100 BTC/day.

Bittrex is a "crypto-just" trade, which means it doesn't enable you to store fiat monetary forms, for example, USD, EUR, GBP, and so on.

They give access to cutting edge exchanging apparatuses like candle graphs and focus, however the UI is very perfect and instinctive, so amateurs ought to have no issues.

8: Poloniex

Established by Tristan D'Agosta, Poloniex has been operational since January 2014 and is without a doubt one of the greatest cryptographic money trades on the planet.

It is based out of the United States and offers +100 digital currencies to its clients to exchange.

At the point when you talk about exchange volumes, nothing beats Poloniex. In 2017, Poloniex had the most noteworthy volume for ETH in light of the fact that it underpins an autonomous Ethereum showcase just as a BTC advertise.

It is a crypto-just trade, however you can begin exchanging effectively by keeping USDT (Tether dollars).

Poloniex additionally has zoomable candle diagrams for 5-minutes, 15-minutes, 30-minutes, 2-hours, 4-hours, and 1-day, alongside a stop-limit highlight for cutting edge digital money dealers.

Poloniex charges an expense of 0.15% to 0.25% on all exchanges relying on whether you are a creator or a taker.

So on the off chance that you are hoping to exchange an assortment of altcoins, at that point you should give Poloniex a shot.

To begin with Poloniex, pursue this official guide.

Keep in mind: As soon as you pursue Poloniex utilizing your email, do try to empower two-factor verification!

Conclusion:

As you make all the way here reading & learning new ways all about to make money from home that is to Utilize your skills and expertise into the work you want to do, the most experience you have in specific work field.

We learned about Graphic Designing and from that we can pick Logo Design as a Most Trending work field that is never going to end ever and along with that having Photoshop skills you can do some good graphic Designing too.

Web Development requires expert people for some big Projects and newbies can also take a part in that work to prove their skills Front end Development is all about Themes and Website Design. So, if you do learn some of these skills you can make some pretty amount on Freelancing platforms,

If you don't have time to Learn skills right now, then you can move forward with the Simple Work Done jobs as a Virtual Assistant and Data Entry Jobs that requires good grip on your work focus in order to Get Done with the Client.

And last but not the least, we discuss about Trading online which includes Bitcoin, Forex Trading. You must invest some money and then Learn some risk management ways to start trading online so that you don't take a loss on your portfolio.
Bitcoin is just like a Digital Gold and it is becoming famous rapidly, so take your chances and Dive Deep into the Skill that suits you the Most.

Thank You for Reading this Book, hope this might get you the Right Success Path.

GOOD LUCK